A Celebration of the 80s

A Celebration of the 80s

Portraits

Photographs and Text by

Nancy Rica Schiff

Introduction by Senator Sam J. Ervin, Jr.

Foreword by Raphael Soyer

Harry N. Abrams, Inc., Publishers, New York

Front cover:
(top, left to right) Sir Rudolf Bing, Isabel Bishop, Raphael Soyer;
(bottom, left to right) Lillian Gish, Aaron Copland, George Burns, Kenneth Burke

Project Director: Barbara Lyons
Editors: Phyllis Freeman, Anne Yarowsky
Designer: Tina Davis Snyder

Library of Congress Cataloging in Publication Data

Schiff, Nancy Rica.
A celebration of the 80s.

1. Photography—Portraits. 2. Aged—Portraits.
I. Title. II. Title: Celebration of the eighties.
TR681.F3S35 1983 779'.23'0924 83-2780
ISBN 0-8109-2276-2 (pbk.)

Published in 1983 by Harry N. Abrams, Incorporated, New York

Printed and bound in Japan

For
my mother and my father
and
my Uncle Arthur

Contents

Introduction

This extraordinary book presents portraits of people who have witnessed many events and who may be thought of as old. Hence, it is not amiss to use this space for a meditation on old age, written by one who has endured for more than fourscore and six years.

Old age has claimed the attention of philosophers and poets since language was invented. What they have said on the subject ranges from the melancholy observations of William Shakespeare's character Jacques in the last scene of *As You Like It* to the joyous words of Robert Browning's character Rabbi Ben Ezra as he extends this invitation to his contemporaries:

> Grow old along with me!
> The best is yet to be,
> The last of life, for which the first was made. . . .

The most impressive panegyric on old age, in my judgment, was written in 150 B.C. by Marcus Tullius Cicero, the eloquent and wise Roman orator, politician, and writer. His essay on old age, *Cato Maior* or *De Senectute,* is available to us in its original Latin or in English translation. In opening his discourse, Cicero, speaking through the character Marcus Cato, says:

> Men who have no resources in themselves for securing a good and happy life find every age burdensome. But those who look for all happiness from within can never think anything bad which nature makes inevitable. In that category before anything else comes old age, to which all wish to attain, and at which all grumble when attained.

These are the four complaints of old age: (1) Old age withdraws us from active employments; (2) Old age enfeebles the body; (3) Old age deprives us of nearly all sensual pleasures; (4) Old age is the next step to death.

No one can gainsay that time ordinarily exacts a heavy toll on those whose lives are long. Since there is an exception to every rule, a few rare persons are exempt from payment of this toll. For example, Moses the Lawgiver "was an hundred and twenty years old when he died: his eye was not dim, nor his natural force abated."

For many years I have undertaken to cultivate a philosophic mind to enable me to confront old age and the sunset of life with calmness and courage. However, before sharing my philosophy with you, I wish to make a few observations. The worth of a life is to be measured by how it is lived, not by the length of its years, months, or days. As Philip James Bailey declared:

> We live in deeds, not years; in thought, not breaths;
> In feelings, not in figures on a dial.
> We should count time by heart-throbs. He most lives
> Who thinks most—feels the noblest—acts the best.

The complaints against old age are at war with the truth proclaimed in Ecclesiastes: "To everything there is a season, and a time to every purpose under the sun." Cicero elaborated further on this theme in his essay on old age:

> The course of life is fixed, and nature admits of its being run but in one way, and only once; and to each part of our life there is something specially seasonable; so that the feebleness of children, as well as the high spirits of youth, the soberness of maturer years, and the ripe wisdom of old age—all have a certain natural advantage which should be secured in its proper season.

At the same time there is more than a modicum of truth in the complaints against old age. Fortunately, however, they do not reveal all of the truth.

Physical strength, which is a prime characteristic of youth, does diminish with the passing of years. Hence, old age weakens our bodies, deprives us of some sensual pleasures, and decreases our capacity to engage in physical activities.

Youth is designated by nature as the time for triumphs of the body. By abstaining from physical vices and living temperately, one can extend the duration of his physical strength and the time for his bodily triumphs.

As the years come and go and physical strength abates, evenhanded nature gives to those who are aging some consolations for what time takes from them. In the words of one poet: "Time still, as he flies, brings increase to her truth,/And gives to her mind what he steals from her youth."

One of these consolations is the realization that the most essential tasks of life are produced by intellectual labor rather than by physical strength or the activity or nimbleness of the body.

Old age must be distinguished from ill health, which may afflict one at any stage of life. Old age does render men more susceptible to accidents and ailments, but it does not ordinarily deny them the pleasures and activities befitting it.

Although old age may rob us of those sensual pleasures that require much vigor, it permits us to enjoy the love of those dear to us, the companionship of our friends, freedom from corroding ambition, tranquillity of thought, music, and the precious memories we have gathered along life's highway. As Alonso of Aragon said, old age gives us the best of four things—old wood to burn, old wine to drink, old friends to trust, and old authors to read.

As we age, life offers us opportunities to acquire the wisdom that only experience teaches and allows us to retain the capacity for intellectual achievement by maintaining our interest in what is happening around us and keeping our minds actively employed.

As long as he retains his mental faculties, a man possesses the most precious gift of God.

In extolling this truth in commencement speeches, I have often said:

> The assertion that God made man just a little lower than the angels finds vindication in the facts that God gave man a brain and placed him in surroundings whose mysteries present a constant challenge to the unceasing employment of that brain. No

man can truly claim that he has as certain possession of learning as of a book or other article of personal property. The world of the mind is an illimitable land whose boundaries are as vast as the universe itself, and thought is calling us at all times to the undiscovered countries lying beyond the next visible range of mountains.

The soothsayers of ancient India exalted an unending search for knowledge in this cryptic phrase: "When thou attainest an hundred years, cease to learn." The Psalmist of old prayed: "So teach us to number our days that we may apply our hearts unto wisdom."

I entreat you to let nothing on this side of the grave put an end to your pursuit of learning. Fortunate, indeed, will you be if you will fondly embrace the belief that knowledge is the most lasting wealth and if you will woo her with such constancy that you will be able to say in modesty and in truth at sunset each day: I am wiser today than I was yesterday. While you may fear that knowledge will become proud because she learns so much, you may be sure that wisdom will always remain humble because she knows so little.

Let books be your friends, for, by so doing, you can summon to your fireside in seasons of loneliness the choice spirits of all the ages. Observe mankind through the eyes of charity, for, by so doing, you will discover anew the oft forgotten fact that earth is peopled with many gallant souls. Study nature, and walk at times in solitude beneath the starry heavens, for, by so doing, you will absorb the great lesson that God is infinite and that your life is just a little beat within the heart of time.

Cling to the ancient landmarks of truth, but be ever ready to test the soundness of a new idea. Accept whatever your mind finds to be true, and whatever your conscience determines to be right, and whatever your heart declares to be noble, even though your act in so doing may drive a hoary prejudice from its throne. And, above all things, meditate often upon the words and deeds of Him who died on Calvary, for, by so doing, "ye shall know the truth, and the truth shall make you free."

Let your life forever harbor at least an echo of Ulysses' inspiring challenge:

> . . . Come, my friends,
> 'Tis not too late to see a newer world.
> Push off, and sitting well in order smite
> The sounding furrows; for my purpose holds
> To sail beyond the sunset, and the baths
> Of all the western stars, until I die. . . .

My philosophy harmonizes with that of Solon, the Athenian statesman and poet, who revealed in one of his poems that he grew older each day learning fresh lessons.

Old age may be, indeed, a time of remarkable accomplishment. Henry Wadsworth Longfellow so testified in his poem *Morituri Salutamus:*

> It is too late! Ah, nothing is too late
> Till the tired heart shall cease to palpitate.
> Cato learned Greek at eighty; Sophocles
> Wrote his grand Oedipus, and Simonides
> Bore off the prize of verse from his compeers,
> When each had numbered more than fourscore years,
> And Theophrastus, at fourscore and ten,
> Had but begun his "Characters of Men."

Chaucer, at Woodstock with the nightingales,
At sixty wrote the Canterbury Tales;
Goethe at Weimar, toiling to the last,
Completed Faust when eighty years were past.
These are indeed exceptions; but they show
How far the gulf-stream of our youth may flow
Into the arctic regions of our lives, . . .
For age is opportunity no less
Than youth itself, though in another dress,
And as the evening twilight fades away
The sky is filled with stars, invisible by day.

If it learns life's lessons well, old age prays this simple prayer: "God grant me the serenity to accept the things I cannot change; the courage to change the things I can; and the wisdom to know the difference."

The fourth complaint against old age—its nearness to death—terrifies many persons of advancing years. To be sure, death cannot be far away from an old man. Nevertheless it claims the babe, the youth, and the middle-aged as well as the old; and no one of any age who is living at noon has any assurance he will survive till sunset.

Since it is appointed for all men to die, common sense ought to teach us that death is inevitable and inescapable, and that there is no more useless folly than wasting one's moments fearing death.

After all, death has only one or the other of two alternative consequences. It either bestows on us an endless forgetfulness in which the wicked cease from troubling and the weary are at rest, or it opens for us the gate to immortality.

I accept the belief in the immortality of man. To be sure, I cannot prove its validity as a scientific fact. I accept it by faith.

As we are rightly informed by Holy Writ, faith is the substance of things hoped for, the evidence of things not seen. Faith enables men and women to walk with confidence in those areas of life that lie outside the bounds of knowledge. Faith is not a storm cellar in which men and women can find refuge from the distresses of life. Faith is instead an inner force that gives them the spiritual strength to face those distresses with calmness and courage.

I likewise cannot demonstrate as a scientific fact that God created man in His own image. I nevertheless know it to be true as I witness the daily devotion of men and women to the causes they cherish and the people they love and when I read the last verse of W. H. Carruth's poem *Each in His Own Tongue:*

> A picket frozen on duty—
>   A mother starved for her brood—
> Socrates drinking the hemlock,
>   And Jesus on the rood;
> And millions who, humble and nameless,
>   The straight, hard pathway plod—
> Some call it Consecration,
>   And others call it God.

I cannot believe that the God who made man in His own image will permit him to perish in the dust.

The desire for immortality is virtually universal. Even Robert G. Ingersoll, the eloquent agnostic, confessed in his oration at his brother's grave: "In the night of Death hope sees a star and listening love hears the rustling of a wing."

The desire for immortality is not to be attributed simply to the egotism of men, or their fear of the unknown beyond the grave, or their repugnance to the thought of their nothingness after death. The philosopher Schopenhauer was sadly in error in his comment that "to desire immortality is to desire the eternal perpetuation of a great mistake." The longing for immortality is prompted by most meritorious motives.

Life on earth at best is all too short and unfinished. Man entertains high hopes for an abundant life with his loved ones and undertakes worthwhile things for them and his generation. His high hopes vanish as he is robbed of those he loves by death, and his hands drop the working tools of life while his undertakings are incomplete.

As a consequence, our hearts cry out that there must be some place after life's fitful fever is over where tears never flow and rainbows never fade, where high hopes are realized and worthy tasks are accomplished, and where those we "have loved long since and lost awhile" stay with us forever.

Revealed religion and an irrepressible intuition of the human heart unite to declare that there is such a place—"an house not made with hands, eternal in the heavens."

We should accept this declaration "in sure and certain hope of the Resurrection to eternal life." After all, there is nothing more miraculous or mysterious in immortality than there is in our life on earth or the existence of the universe.

These considerations should prompt us to accept this admonition of William Cullen Bryant's *Thanatopsis:*

> So live, that when thy summons comes to join
> The innumerable caravan, which moves
> To that mysterious realm, where each shall take
> His chamber in the silent halls of death,
> Thou go not, like the quarry-slave at night,
> Scourged to his dungeon, but, sustained and soothed
> By an unfaltering trust, approach thy grave,
> Like one that wraps the drapery of his couch
> About him, and lies down to pleasant dreams.

We shall not know while we abide here what the "house not made with hands, eternal in the heavens" is like or what our way of life will be after we pass its threshold. We can hope, however, that these things have been portrayed with some prophetic foresight by Rudyard Kipling in his poem *When Earth's Last Picture Is Painted:*

> When Earth's last picture is painted and the tubes are
>   twisted and dried,
> When the oldest colours have faded, and the youngest
>   critic has died,
> We shall rest, and, faith, we shall need it—lie down
>   for an aeon or two,
> Till the Master of All Good Workmen shall put us to
>   work anew.
>
> And those that were good shall be happy: they shall
>   sit in a golden chair;
> They shall splash at a ten-league canvas with brushes
>   of comets' hair;
> They shall find real saints to draw from—Magdalene,
>   Peter, and Paul;
> They shall work for an age at a sitting, and never be tired
>   at all!
> And only The Master shall praise us, and only The
>   Master shall blame;
> And no one shall work for money, and no one shall
>   work for fame,
> But each for the joy of the working, and each, in his
>   separate star,
> Shall draw the Thing as he sees It for the God of
>   Things as They are!

Sam J. Ervin, Jr.
Former U.S. Senator

Foreword

This book began with me. While posing, Nancy would snap my picture during rest periods. Then the thought occurred to young Nancy Rica Schiff to do a book on octogenarians, and I was impressed by her great interest in the people she photographed and the energetic, intelligent way she went about carrying out this project.

I am now eighty-three years old (twenty years older than Rembrandt was when he died) and am still working. When people ask me, "Are you still painting, Mr. Soyer?" it's like being asked "Are you still breathing?"

The people in this book are all eighty and over. Sixty - two octogenarians—writers, poets, painters, musicians, actors, politicians, sports people, etc.—all actively engaged in their professions, all feeling, I'm sure, that life without their work would be meaningless. Even though to outlive one's contemporaries is sad, there is still a sense of triumph in living long.

Many books on various aspects and themes of photography are being published these days. *A Celebration of the 80s* is an homage to active old age.

Raphael Soyer

Aaron Copland

November 14, 1900

Nothing in Aaron Copland's background could have suggested that he would one day become the composer of such American classics as the three ballets *Billy the Kid, Rodeo,* and *Appalachian Spring.* The son of Eastern European immigrants, Copland vividly remembers his storekeeper father's bewilderment when he announced that he was going to be a composer. When asked if he was glad he had made that decision, Copland came back with an emphatic "Hell, yes!"

He is a distinguished conductor, pianist, and author, and a tireless promoter of the works of other American composers as well.

So absorbed in music is Copland that, waiting for me to take my pictures, he became immersed in the score I had placed in his hand as a prop. Humming his way through the score, he was completely oblivious to what was going on.

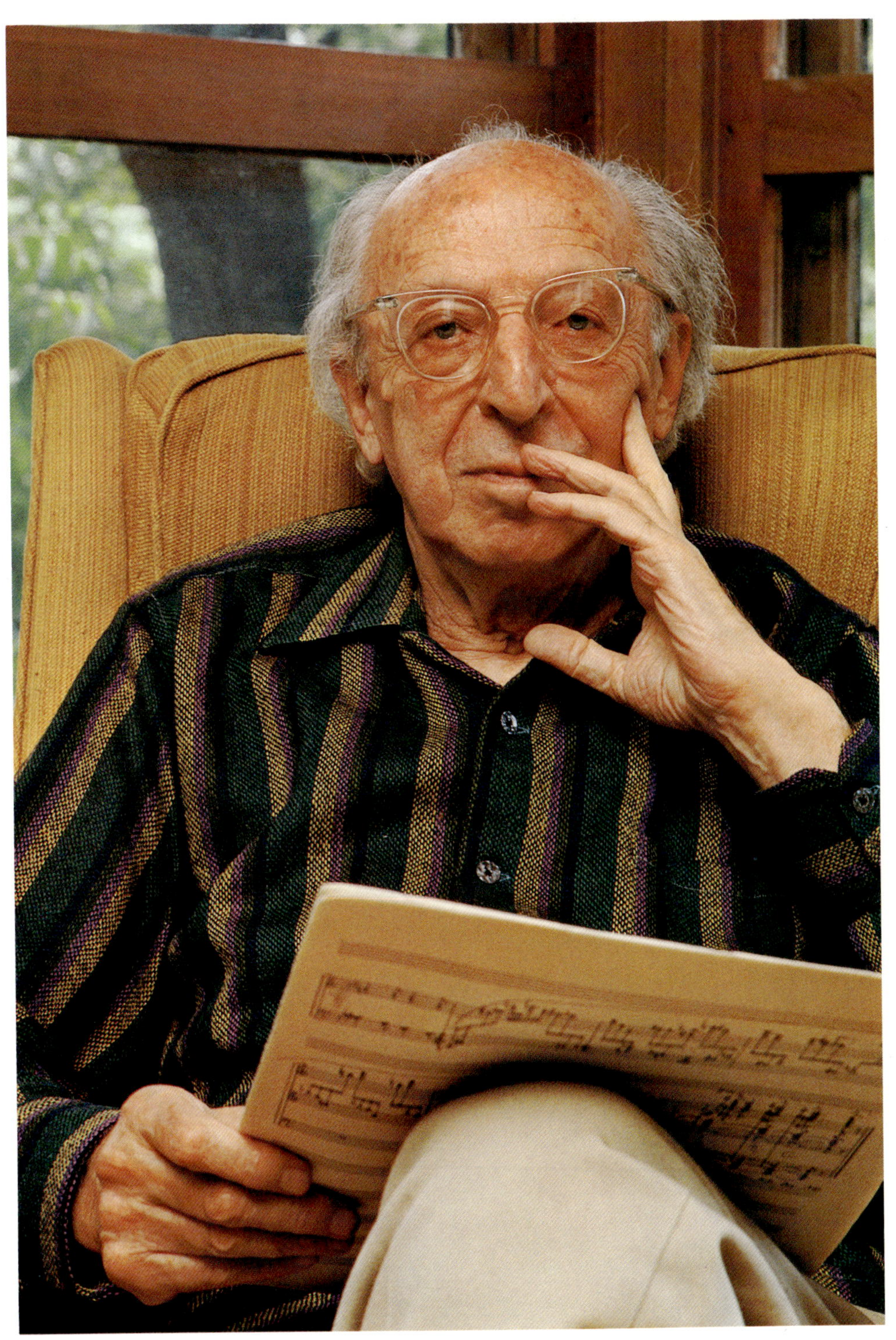

Reuben Nakian

August 10, 1897

I draw all the time,'' said Reuben Nakian, who had just closed his most recent one-man show in New York. ''Art, you know, is ninety-five percent drawing. If you don't have the human concept, if you don't have the human figure, if there isn't great drawing—then to me it's not art, it's just decoration.''

The sculpture that has made Nakian famous bears no resemblance to the abstract modern art he so disdains. It is as alive, as vital—and as human—as the artist himself. Nakian started to sculpt at the age of ten; seventy-odd years later he is still perfecting, refining, and growing.

Nakian is uncompromising about art—what is good and what is bad. He is equally passionate about other aspects of life, but is gentled by a wonderful ability to laugh at himself.

Several times during our photo session I told him he looked angry. ''Good,'' he replied. ''I like to look tough, because really I'm soft.'' Then he explained, ''I'm tough in art—but I'm soft in life.''

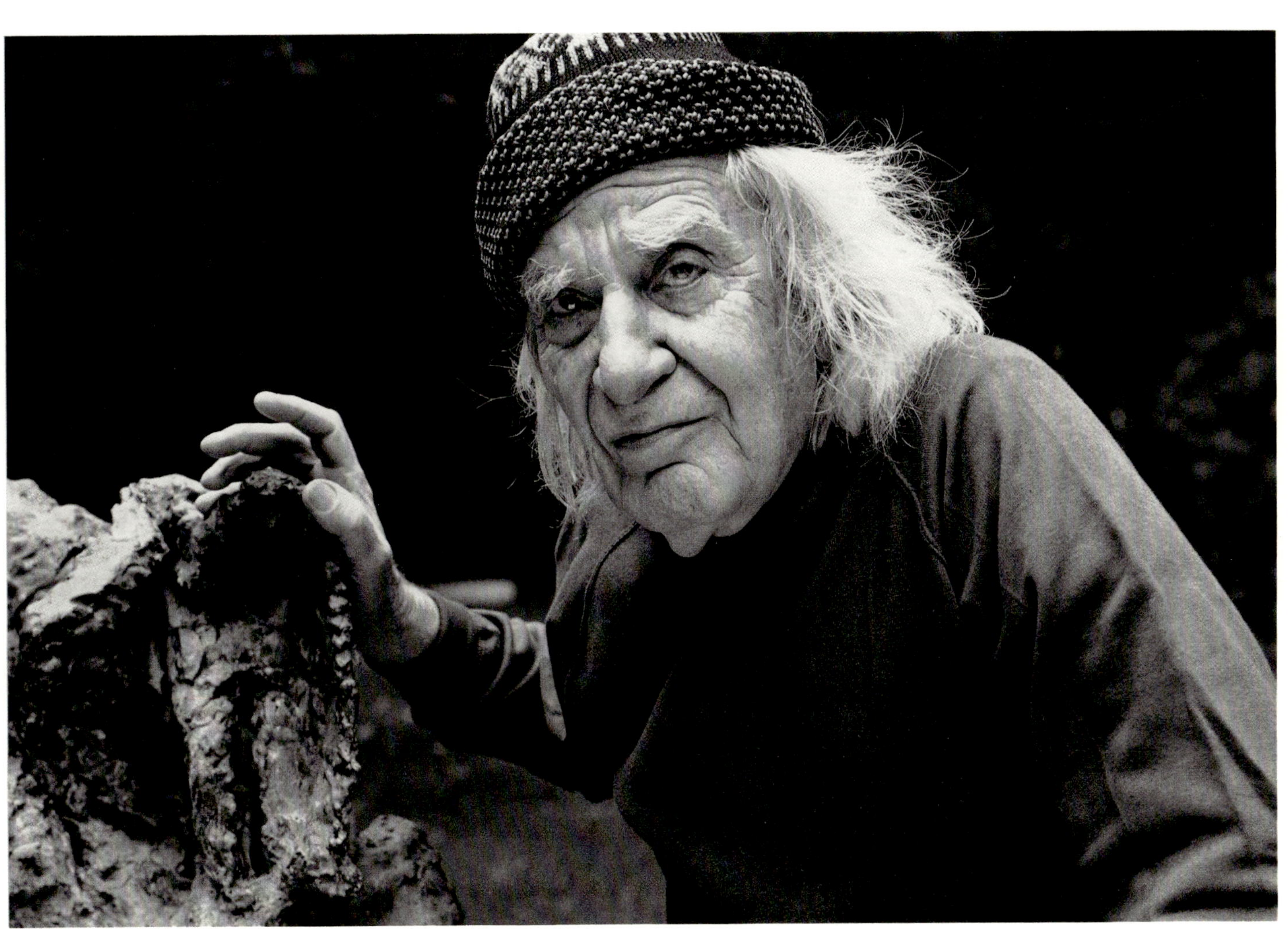

Lillian Gish

October 14, 1896

Lillian Gish's New York apartment was originally her mother's—a rare example of continuity in a city known for its continually shifting population. The rooms are filled with wonderful family pictures; the one I loved was an exquisite hand-tinted photograph of Lillian and her late sister, Dorothy.

On a fateful day in 1912, Lillian and Dorothy Gish were introduced to the director D. W. Griffith; the very same day both girls acted in their first film, Griffith's *An Unseen Enemy.* It marked the start of a decade of collaboration between Lillian and the director, which resulted in the legendary *Birth of a Nation,* as well as many other memorable films.

Lillian Gish, often called the greatest dramatic actress of the silent screen, left Hollywood in 1930 and returned to her first love, the stage. She has continued to appear regularly on the stage, TV, and screen.

Clearly a professional in photographic matters, Miss Gish had one major direction in our photo session. She insisted that the camera always be at eye level or above—a device that, like her white dress, is intended to enhance her doll-like beauty.

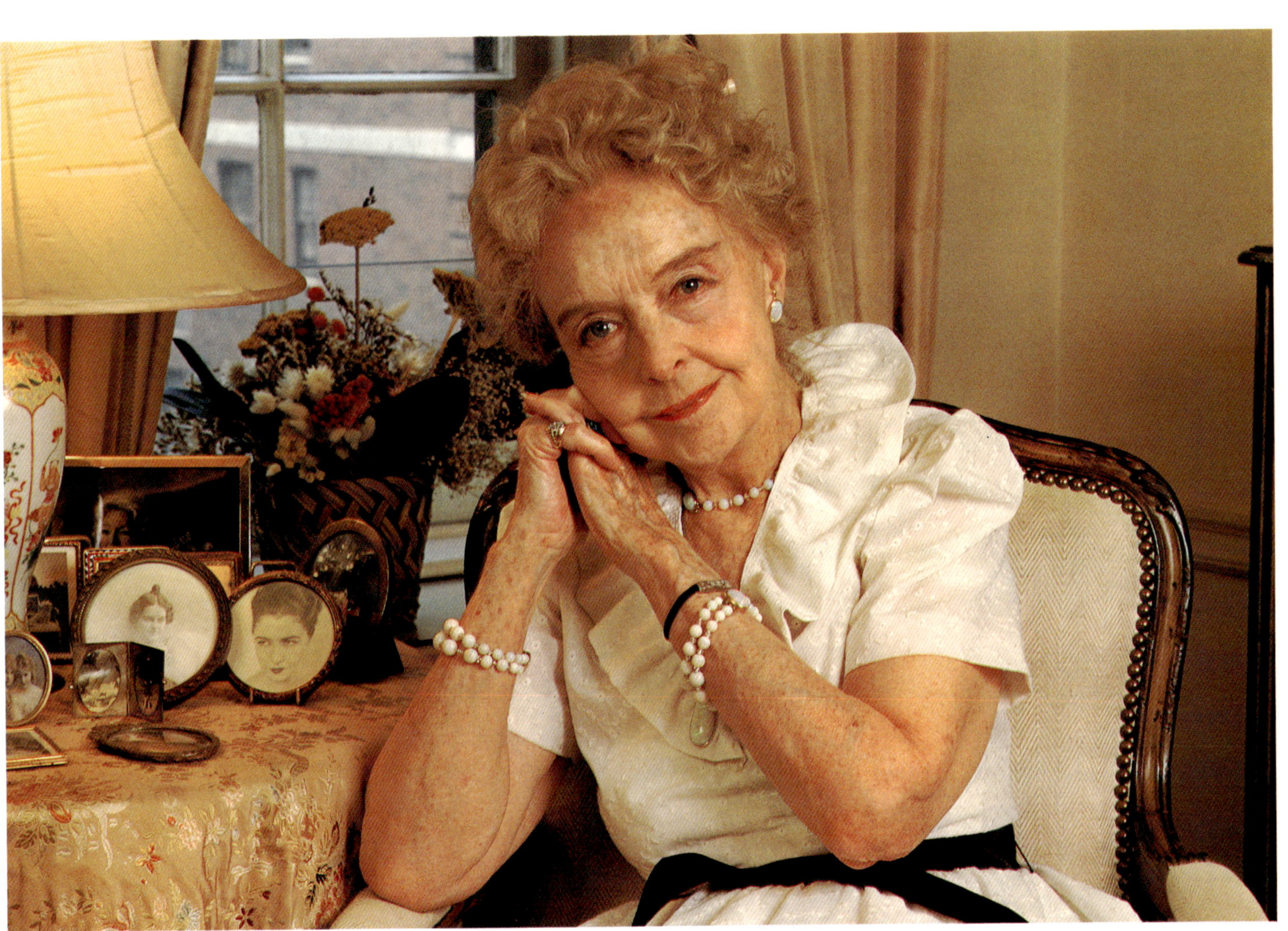

V. S. Pritchett

December 16, 1900

Victor Sawdon Pritchett went to work at sixteen in the London leather trade. Four years later he scraped together his savings and fled to Paris, determined to be a writer. Once there he recalls that "like most young writers, I couldn't think what to write about"—until it occurred to him that "this very moment" was his subject. From that point on he began writing sketches of the life he saw around him.

V. S. Pritchett is widely considered the preeminent critic of fiction in English today. But while his criticism, nonfiction books, memoirs, and novels have won him wide acclaim—short stories remain his real interest in life.

Pritchett's writing and conversation are marked by a delightful sense of humor and irony. The literary essays that have brought him fame are dismissed as a "lazy job" because, he says, they use other people's ideas. On the other hand, Pritchett feels that short-story writing is "full of glooms and depressions—but an enormous satisfaction when you are finished." "And," he adds with a grin, "it's colossal if people like it."

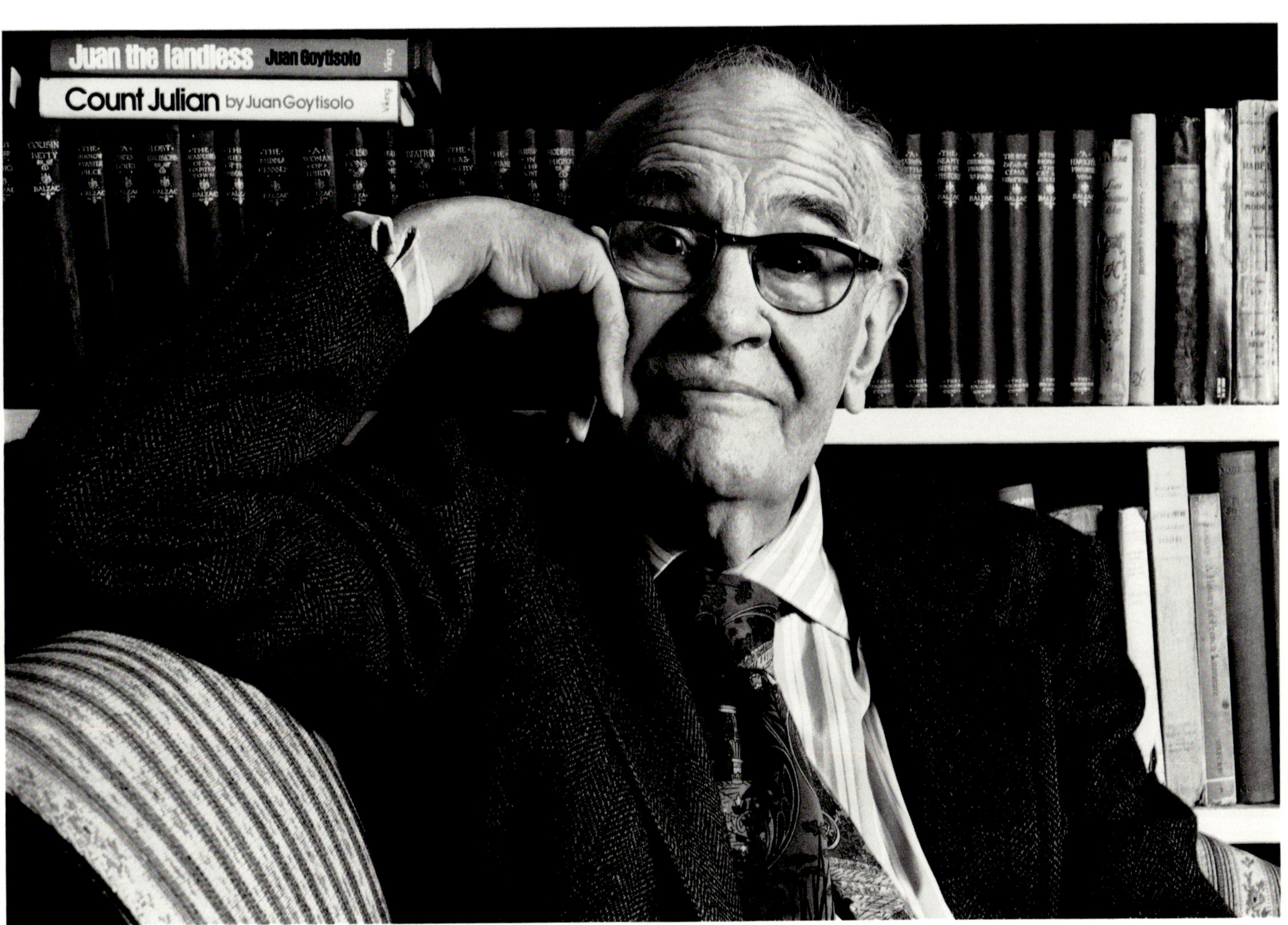
Juan the landless Juan Goytisolo
Count Julian by Juan Goytisolo

R. Buckminster Fuller

July 12, 1895

Often called a "modern-day Leonardo da Vinci," R. Buckminster Fuller has his own term for himself. He is, in Bucky Fuller Language, a "comprehensivist," a man whose work and vision encompass all aspects of the human race, and what he calls Spaceship Earth and Universe. He is an architect, inventor, philosopher, mathematician, scientist, engineer, cartographer, poet, environmentalist, world planner, and educator.

Although he completed less than two years of college and floundered until his thirties, Bucky Fuller is the recipient of honorary degrees, awards, and academic appointments. He is a wondrous inventor, and his publications number in the hundreds. His designs—of which the geodesic dome is merely the most famous—are based on the conservation of energy and materials.

For those desiring a glimpse of this "comprehensivist's" understanding of his life, work, and Spaceship Earth, a forty-three-hour videotape of Bucky "thinking out loud"—made on a dare during his eightieth year—is presented at seminars for two hundred fifty dollars.

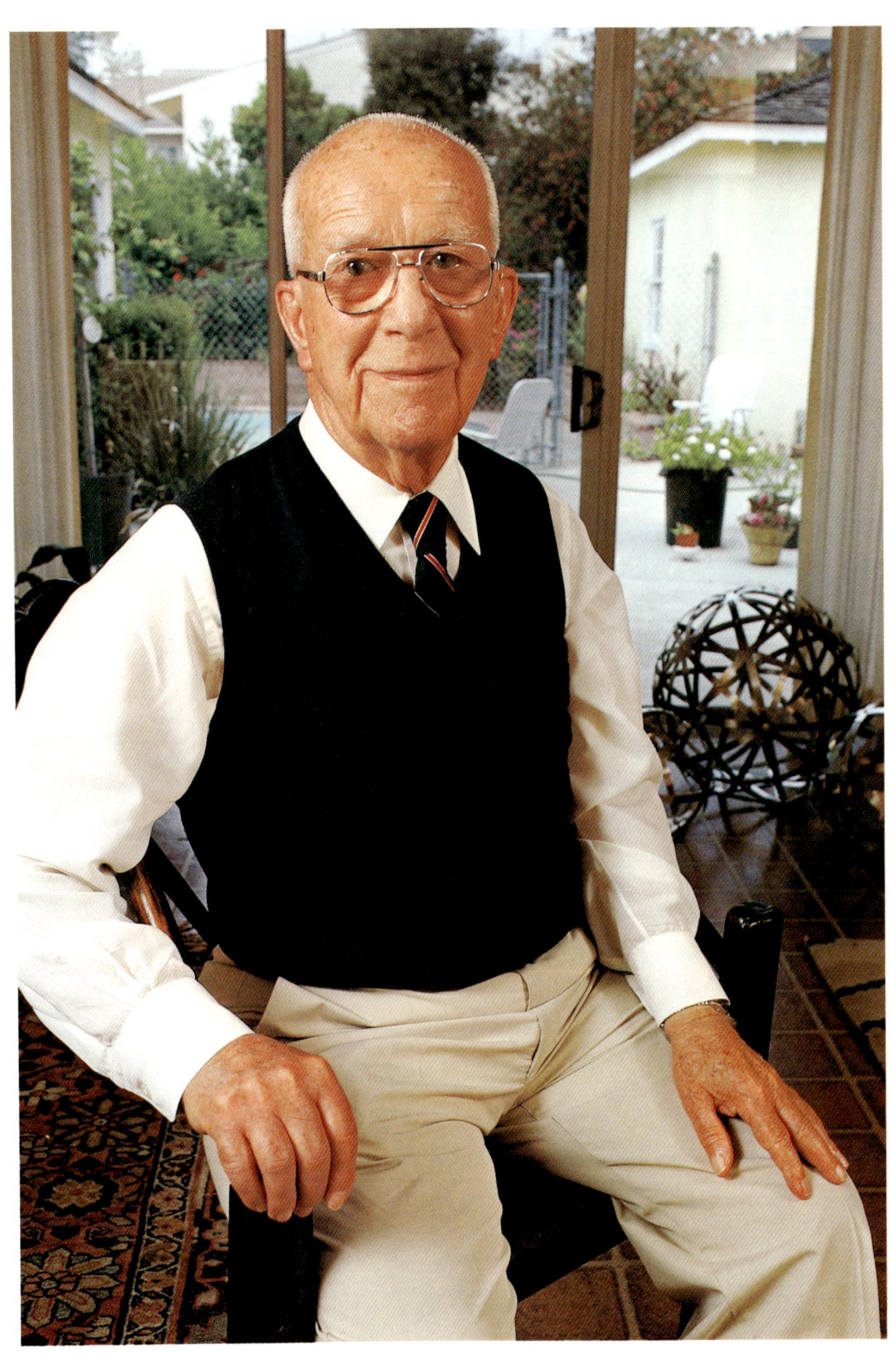

Henry Steele Commager

October 25, 1902

"That's it. Very nice. Beautiful . . . beautiful," I intoned, as is my habit, peering through the lens at Henry Steele Commager—the shutter clicking away. "That's hardly an accurate choice of adjectives," the dean of American historians rejoined, an impish grin creasing his face.

Henry Steele Commager has little time to enjoy the glory that has accrued to him through a half-century of work interpreting United States history to his fellow Americans. Recently asked to what he ascribes his success, Commager replied, "Any man of my age who deludes himself into believing he is a success ought to be in an asylum."

A bouncing, exuberant scholar with a perennially questing mind, he fits perfectly my image of the absentminded professor. Amherst College's usual retirement age of sixty-seven has been indefinitely suspended for Henry Steele Commager. He continues to teach and to write—currently working on three books at the same time.

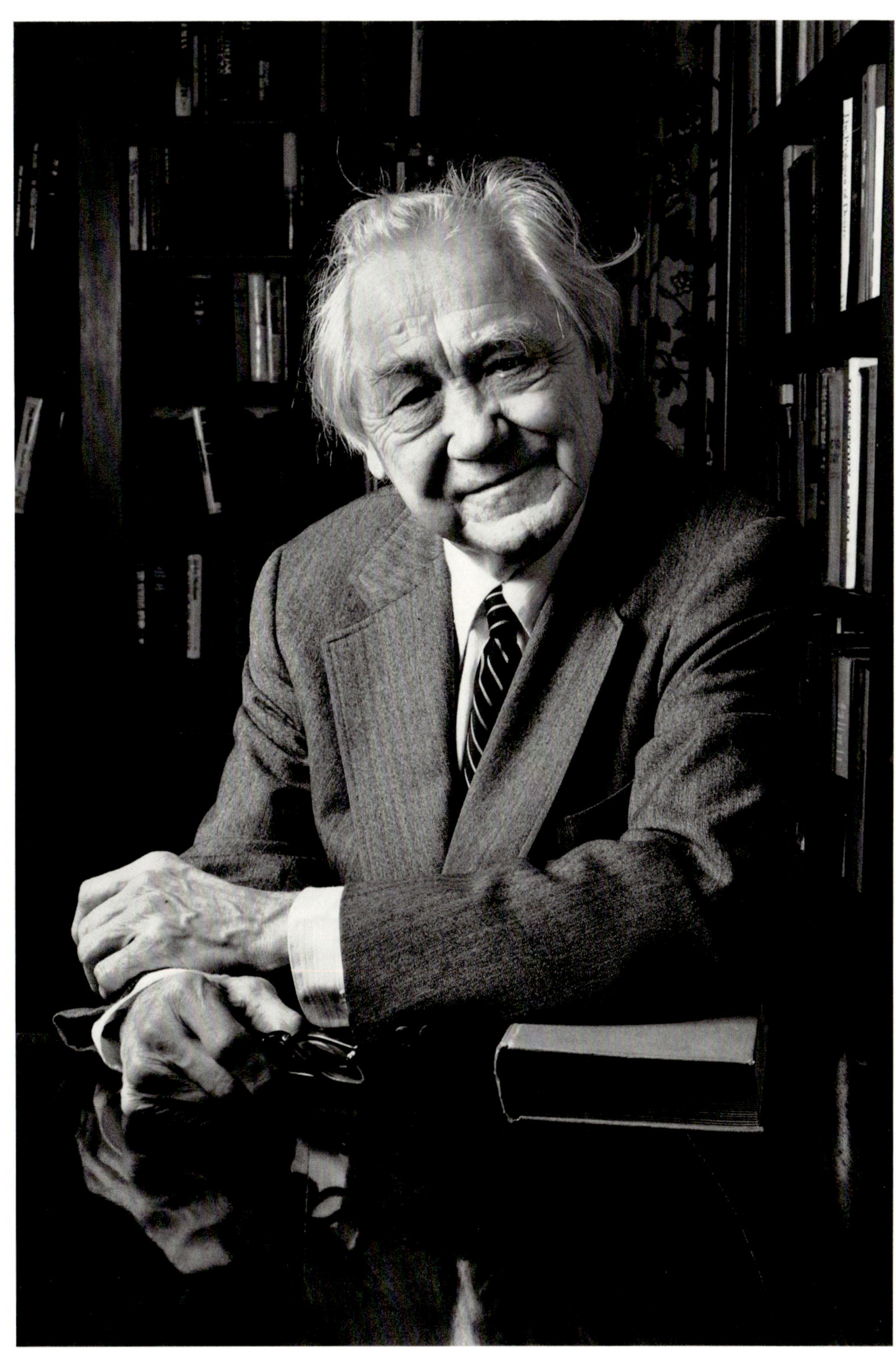

Sidney Janis

July 8, 1896

Gallery owner and art connoisseur Sidney Janis started out as a shirt manufacturer in the 1920s. His knowledge of art was completely self-acquired, his interest dating back to those early business trips to New York when he would while away free time in the city's art galleries.

Successful in business, he sold his interest in 1939 and "retired" to devote himself to writing, collecting art, and organizing museum exhibitions. When he ran low on funds a decade later, he decided to combine the passion of his life with making money and opened the prestigious gallery that bears his name.

Sidney Janis amassed one of the world's most important private collections of modern art, spanning new waves in art and including Pop Art. In 1967 he gave the collection to The Museum of Modern Art in New York City.

Far from retired, he is the first to arrive at and the last to leave the Sidney Janis Gallery on New York's Fifty-seventh Street. In his spare time he is at work on his memoirs.

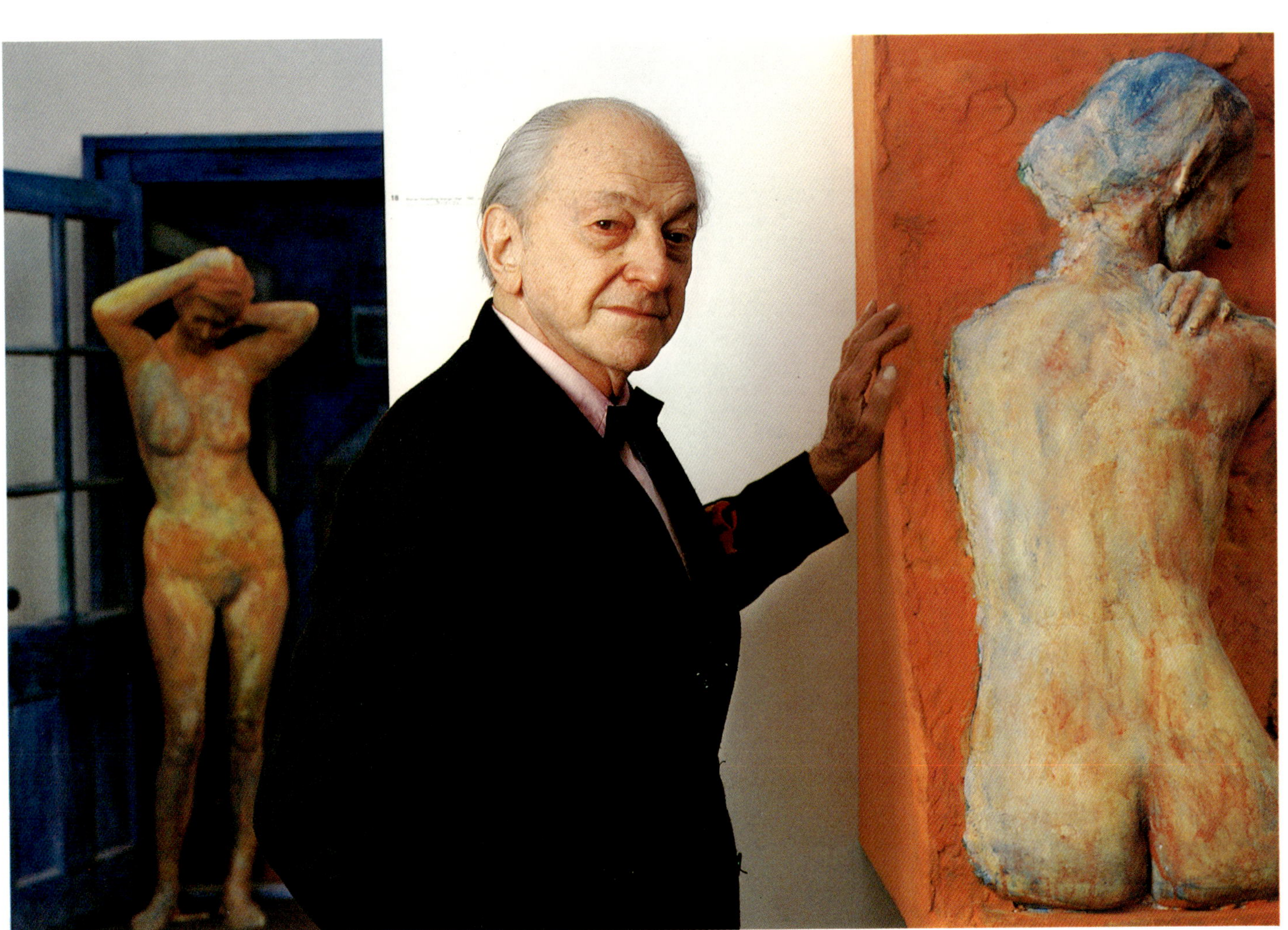

Frances Goodrich

December 21, 1895

Albert Hackett

February 16, 1900

Frances Goodrich and Albert Hackett have been married for close to fifty-two years and have collaborated on more than thirty-five films and a number of plays.

The Hacketts started out as actors. They met on the Broadway stage, married, and went to Hollywood to make their fortunes as screenwriters. They wrote *The Thin Man,* based on the original story by Dashiell Hammett, *Seven Brides for Seven Brothers, Easter Parade,* and more than thirty other screenplays. Frances says: "In order to see all our films, you would have to be an insomniac."

New York is their true home, and they returned to the East to write for the stage. For Broadway they adapted *The Diary of Anne Frank*, for which they won numerous awards, including the Pulitzer Prize.

Being with this couple is like watching the rehearsal of a comedy team. She calls him "Hackett," murmuring, "Albert never suited him" in an aside. Unvarnished honesty and noisy fights mark their collaboration. "We can't work with other writers," they say. "Being polite is too much of a strain."

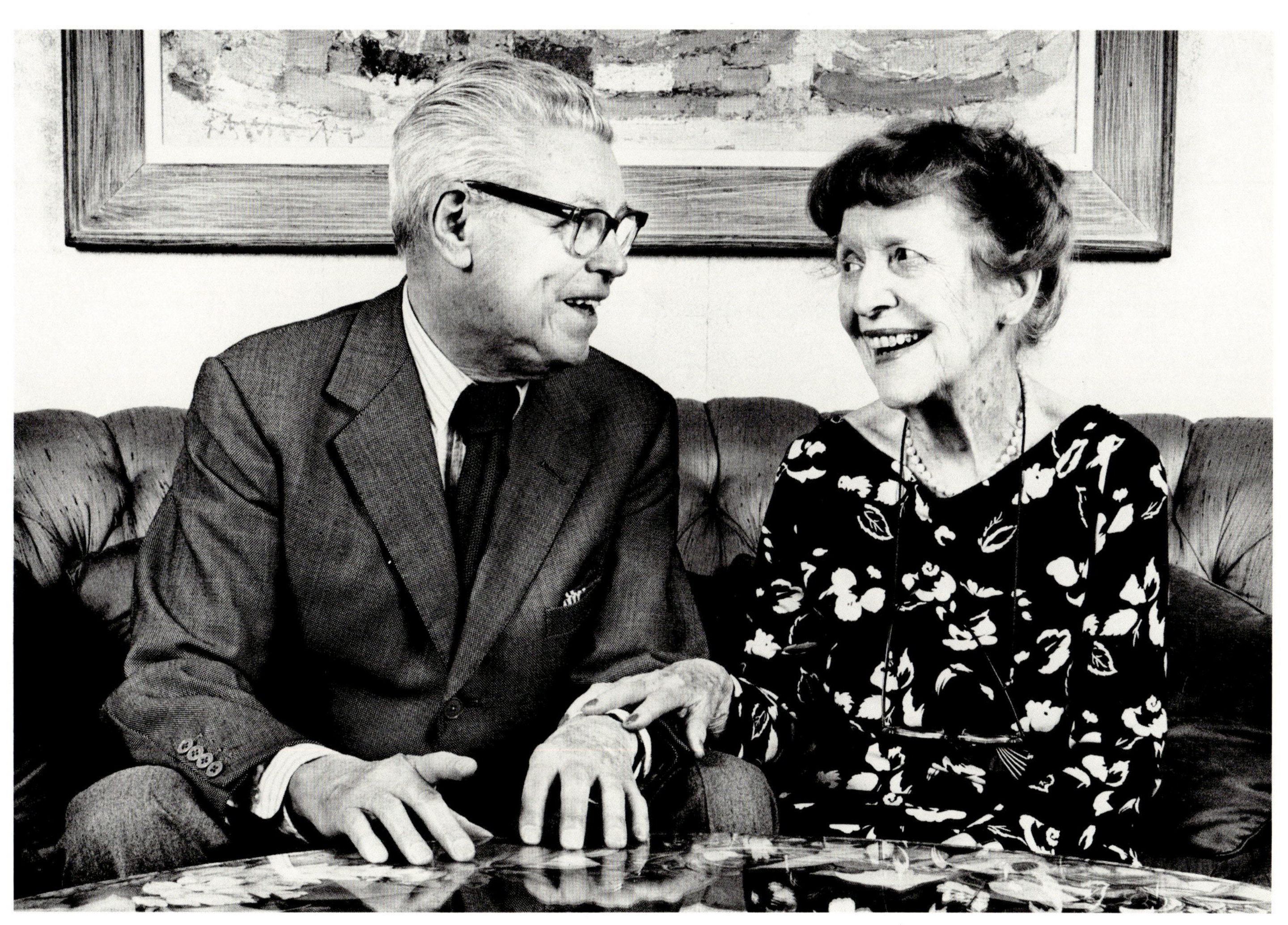

Ruth Page

March 22, 1900

I think I must have started dancing in my mother's womb,'' says Ruth Page. Eighty-three years later she is still dancing. She continues to exercise daily, teaches a choreography class at her School of the Dance in Chicago, travels around the country working with ballet companies as guest choreographer, and has recently taken up tap dancing.

Ruth Page has worked with the world's foremost dancers and ballet companies as well as formed several companies of her own. Innovative and versatile, she has danced and choreographed everything from jazz to classical ballet. *The Merry Widow,* one of the operettas that she choreographed as a ballet, was first performed in 1955; it remains an enduring favorite.

A photographer's ideal model, Ruth Page is constantly in motion—dancing through an endless variety of poses that imbue each photograph with its own distinct and vibrant mood.

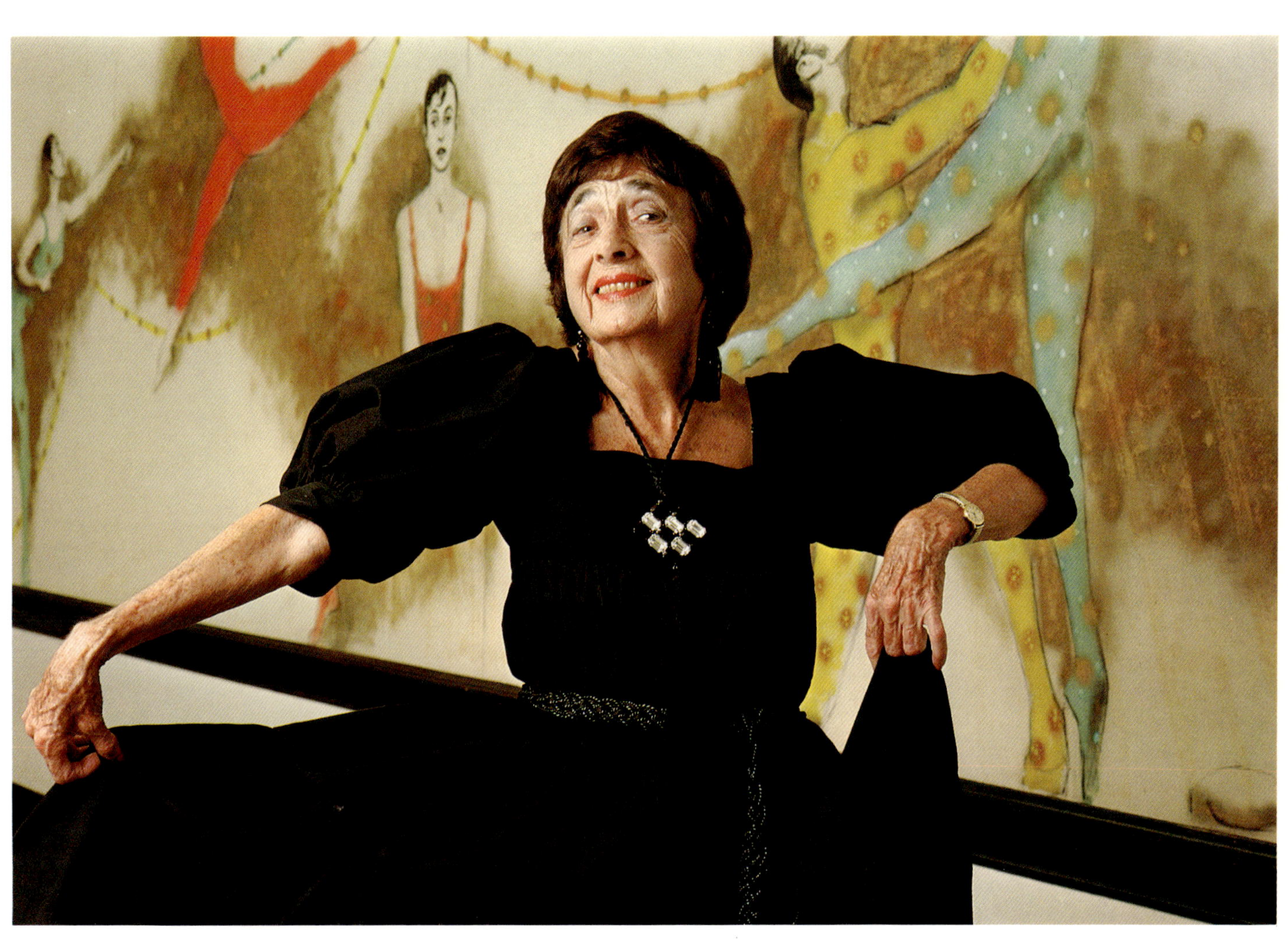

Meridel Le Sueur

February 22, 1900

A thoroughly midwestern American radical, raised in an ardent socialist home, Meridel Le Sueur wrote to me:

"I was born at the beginning of the century, the most brutal and bloody one, in a white puritan house in Murray, Iowa; a loving mixture of American immigrant matings, of dissenters, democrats, radicals, utopians, and the young strangers who kept coming on for the struggle, furling out new strengths and bright mutations, in defense of life against death."

Blacklisted during the McCarthy period, unpublished for decades, Meridel Le Sueur has just been "found." Her writing—writing that was too radical, too feminist for her time—writing that conveys the anger and despair of the dispossessed of America—is today being published to wide critical acclaim. Still passionate, idealistic, and committed, she continues—as she did during her decades of obscurity—to travel throughout the country, to seek out new people, and always to write.

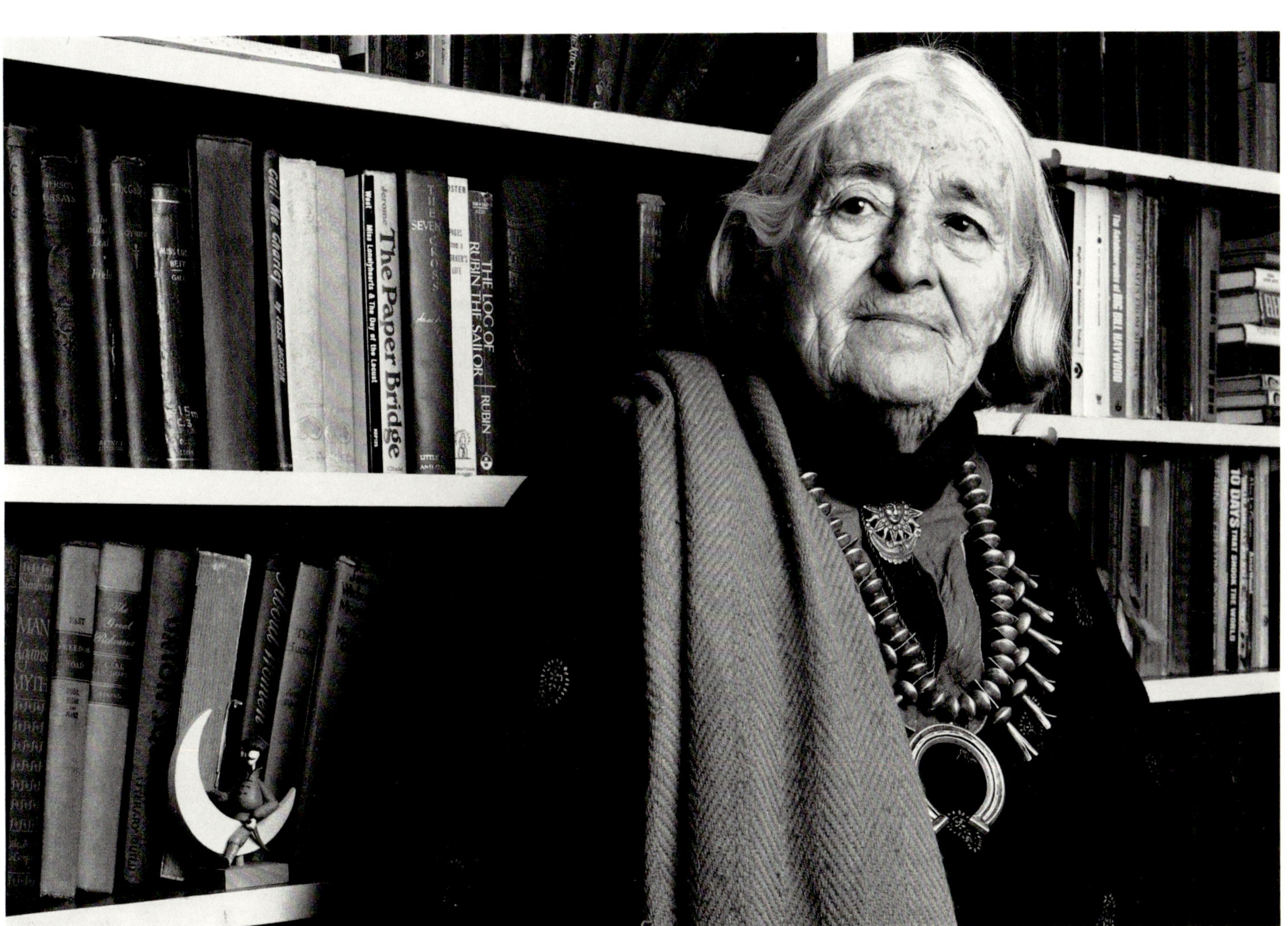
The Paper Bridge
Miss Lonelyhearts & The Day of the Locust
THE SEVEN
THE LOG OF RUBIN THE SAILOR
RUBIN

Hermione Gingold

December 9, 1897

There are some women whose voices are never forgotten. With her deep, throaty tone, British accent, and pithy remarks, Hermione Gingold is one of these. She came to the United States from England in 1954. A major impetus for her move, she maintains, was provided by U.S. servicemen, who were the most enthusiastic audiences for her shows during World War II.

Since then she has acted in numerous plays on and off Broadway, appeared on TV talk shows, written three books, made several recordings from *Lysistrata* to *Peter and the Wolf,* received a Grammy and a Golden Globe Award, and played the worldly-wise grandmother in the movie *Gigi.*

Hermione describes her apartment on Manhattan's East Side as a "bazaar"; every available inch is filled with statues, throw pillows, knickknacks, and assorted cultural oddities. She and I quickly found common ground in our shared fondness for chocolate and concern about weight. "Just last night," she confided, "I had no dinner—and ate this divine chocolate marzipan instead."

Like many of her fellow octogenarians, Hermione relishes the company of young people—and for her that often means male and handsome.

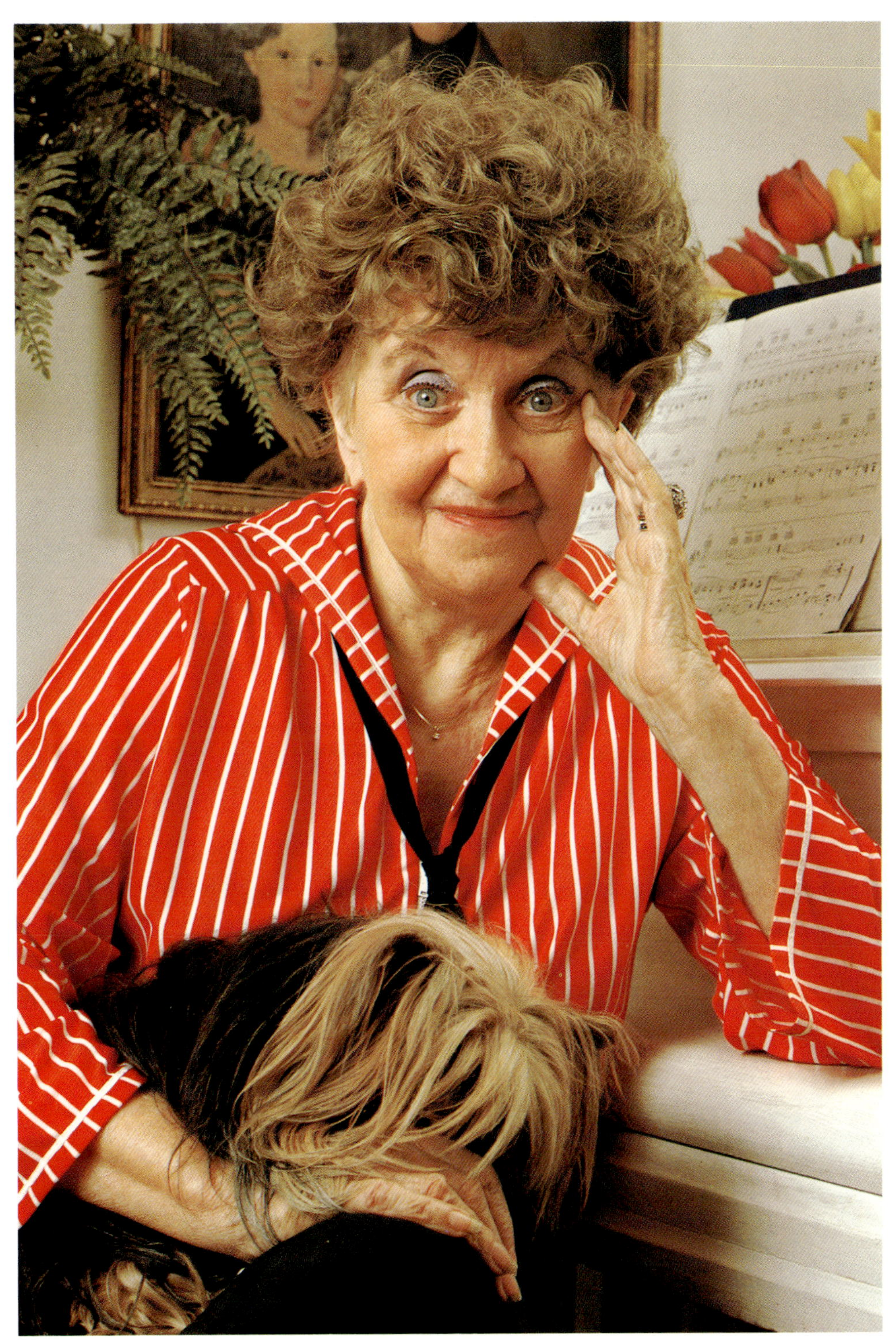

Claude Pepper

September 8, 1900

No book of octogenarians would be complete without Claude Pepper, the spokesman for elderly Americans on Capitol Hill.

Pepper was elected to the United States Senate from Florida in 1936. A liberal Democrat, he lost his 1950 reelection bid at the height of the McCarthy era. In 1962 Claude Pepper won election to the U.S. Congress as a representative from the Miami area, a seat he has retained ever since. Assured of reelection, Pepper spent the 1982 campaign season appearing in twenty-seven states around the country on behalf of other Democrats.

Claude Pepper talked to me about the problems he most wants solved: Social Security, crime, school dropouts. Admitting that if he had retired he probably wouldn't be alive today, he added with his Southern humor, "I am as full of ideas about what to do in the future as a dog has fleas."

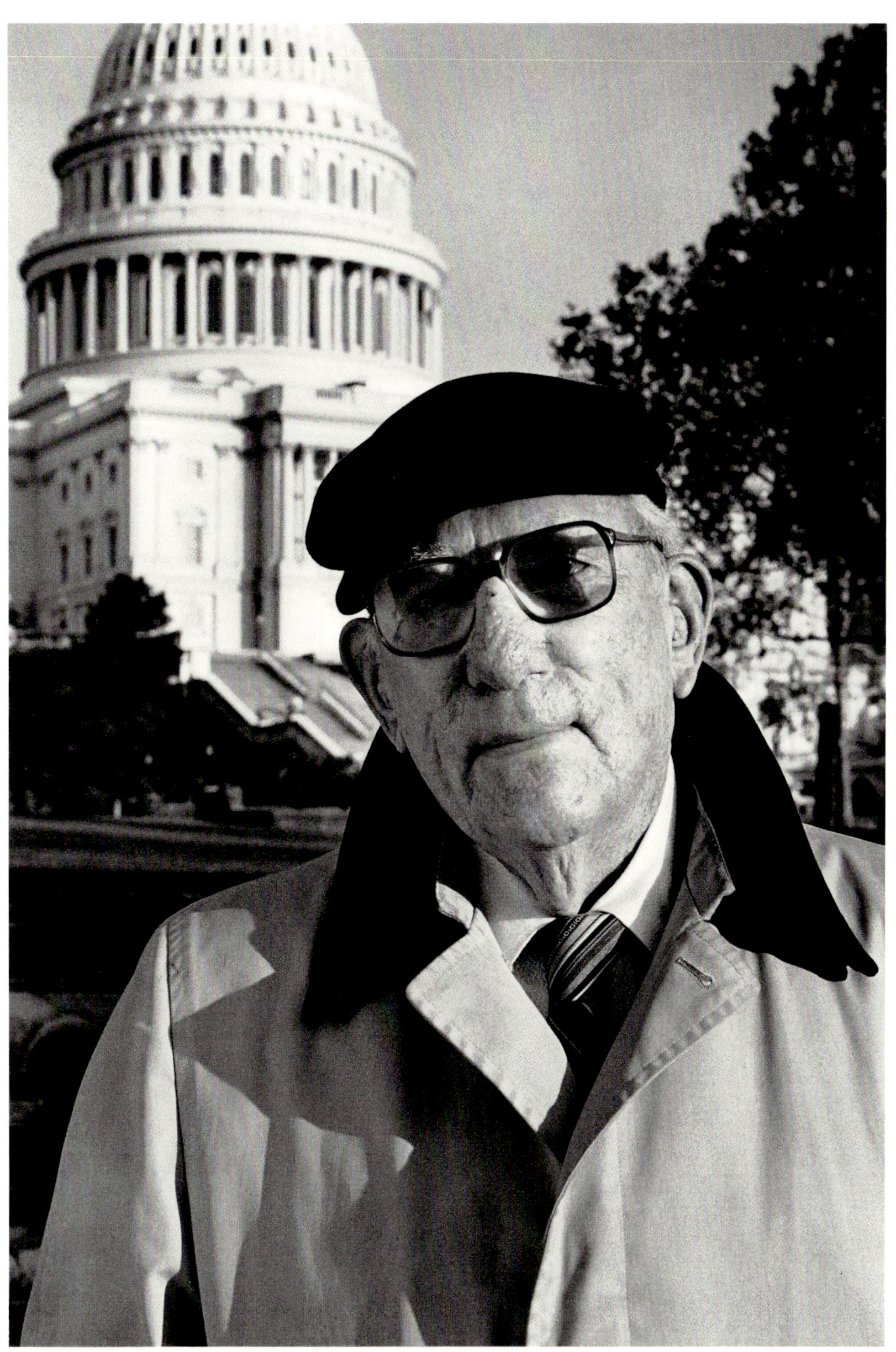

Al Hirschfeld

June 21, 1903

Al Hirschfeld is the master doodler whose theatrical caricatures are recognized by millions. After sixty years of freelancing for the *New York Times,* he says his start was accidental. As a young man he had gone to the theater with a press agent who observed him sketching on his program. The press agent—surprised at Hirschfeld's unexpected talent—said he would try to place the drawing somewhere. The following week it appeared in the *Herald Tribune.* Then the *Times* called, and before long he was working for several newspapers.

For Al Hirschfeld, drawing is as natural as eating or walking. He never wanted to do anything else. He says that he has spent most of his life trying to find out what makes a line go a certain way and why it communicates itself to a viewer. When I asked him if he had found the answer, he said, "No. If I ever found an answer, it wouldn't be an art—it would be a science."

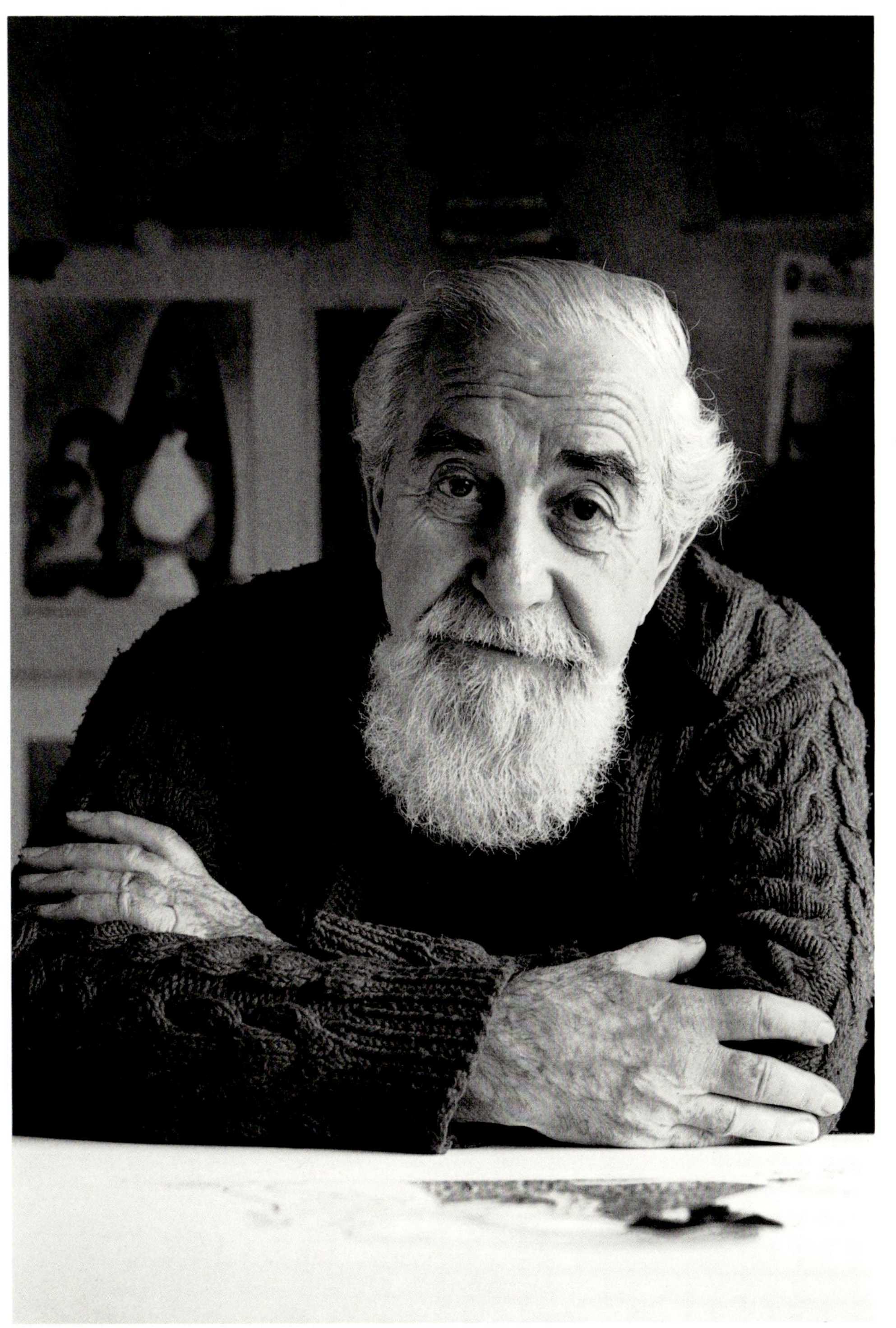

Andrés Segovia

February 18, 1893

When Andrés Segovia was in New York recently, I arranged to photograph him at the end of a master class he was giving. As he left the stage, Segovia was deluged by members of the audience with requests for autographs, photographs, or just a few words. He could not say no to any of them. Finally I said to him, "Señor Segovia, I'm going to kidnap you," and I extricated him from the crowd.

Andrés Segovia is the man who created for the classical guitar a place on the world's concert stages that few people believed the instrument could ever attain. He commissioned new works and adapted forgotten pieces.

One of those rare artists who transcends his instrument, his music, and his time, Segovia is an international legend—his name alone able to fill the largest concert hall anywhere in the world.

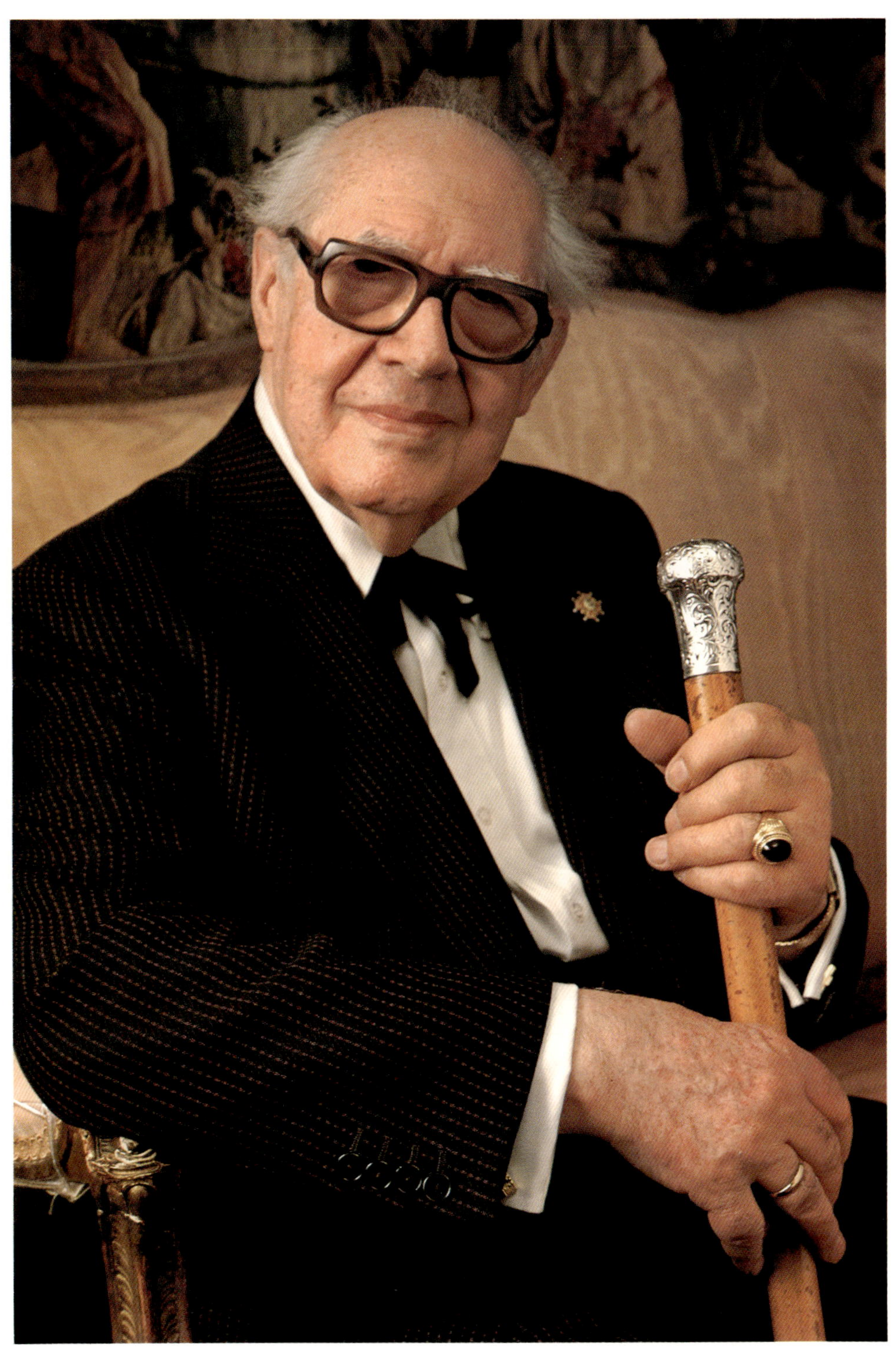

Pietro Belluschi

August 18, 1899

Pietro Belluschi's Portland, Oregon, home is a house he designed for a client, never thinking it would one day be his. The house, situated on a cliff overlooking the city, embodies the eloquent simplicity characteristic of all his work.

Belluschi grew up in Rome and came to the United States on a university scholarship in 1923. Over the ensuing decades he became one of America's most distinguished architects. His designs range from single-family homes, often of wood, in the Northwest to gleaming postwar churches and major private and public buildings on both coasts. Belluschi served as a consultant on the Pan Am Building in New York City, and his designs for The Juilliard School of Music and Alice Tully Hall have been acclaimed as outstanding components of the city's Lincoln Center complex.

Pietro Belluschi is the personification of elegance and charm. He explained, "At the final stage of one's life, a wise man had better count his blessings if he wishes to exorcise the creeping indignities of old age."

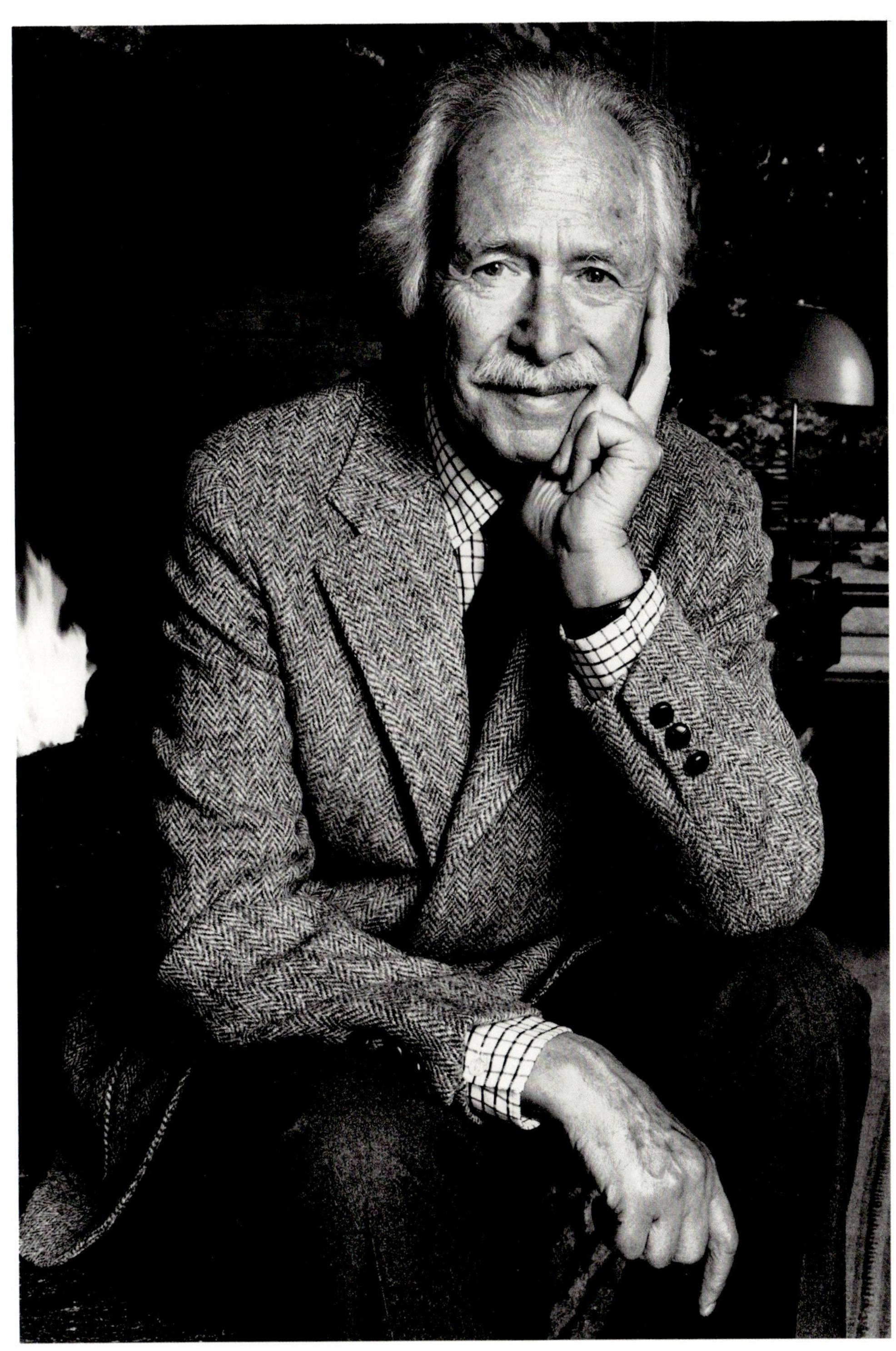

Lloyd Goodrich

July 10, 1897

In 1933 Lloyd Goodrich published his first book, a biography of the American painter Thomas Eakins. Fifty years later, two volumes of his current critical study of Eakins have been published, and he has almost completed work on the third and final volume.

Lloyd Goodrich started out to be a painter. Concluding that painting was not his primary talent, he turned to art criticism and museum work. He spent thirty-seven years with the Whitney Museum of American Art in New York City, serving as its director for ten of those years.

Author of the pioneering appraisal of Edward Hopper's career as an artist, Lloyd Goodrich is responsible for the Whitney Museum's unparalleled collection of Hopper works—paintings, drawings, and notebooks. He is pictured here standing in front of Edward Hopper's *Early Sunday Morning*.

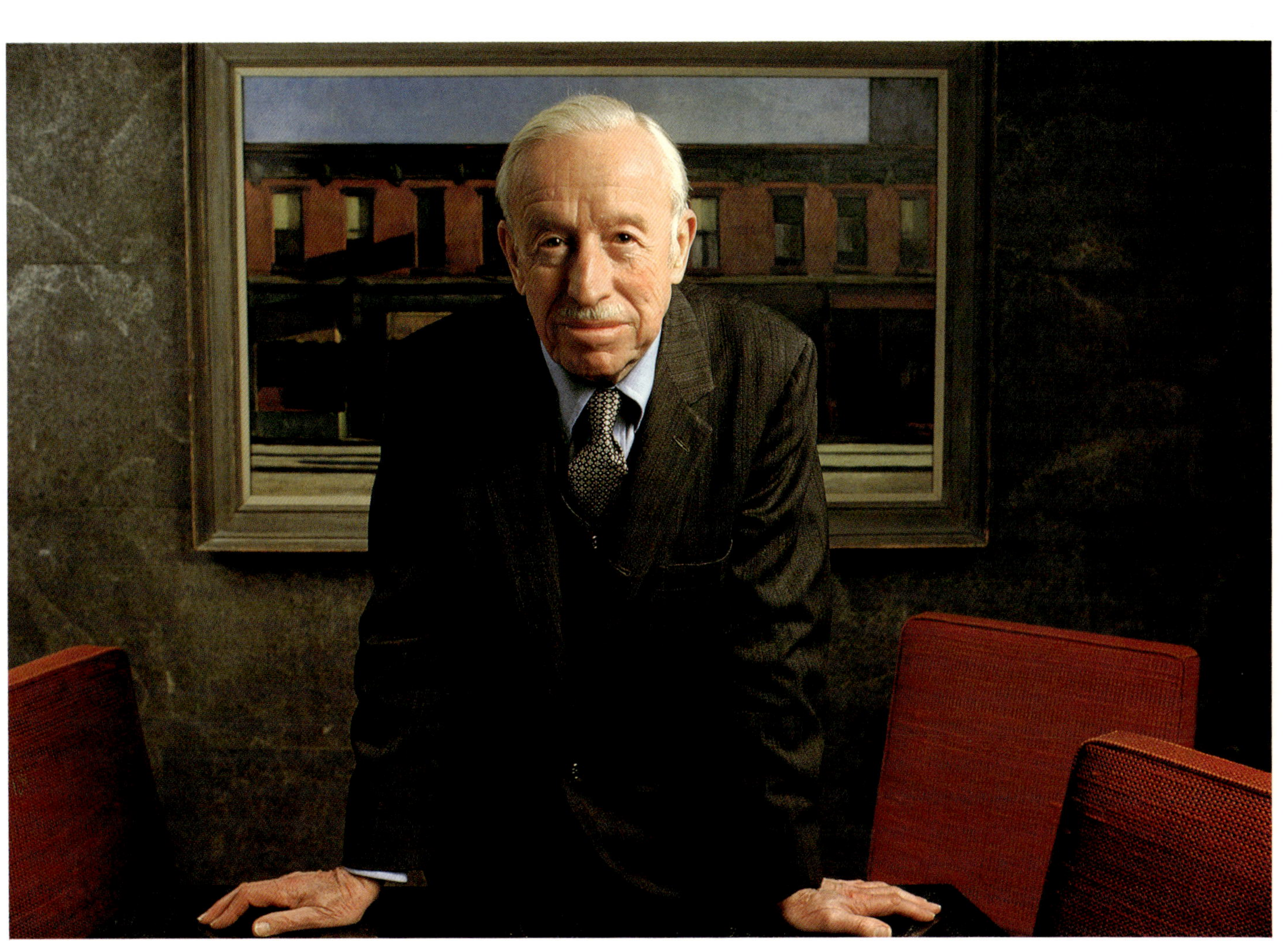

Eva LeGallienne

January 11, 1899

"I wasn't the first Peter Pan," remarked Eva LeGallienne, "but I was the first to fly to the balcony!" That was in 1928, and in 1982 she flew again as the White Queen in her third production of *Alice in Wonderland.*

Eva LeGallienne made her stage debut in London at the age of fourteen. Two years later she came to New York, and by the early 1920s she had become one of Broadway's leading stars: talented, beautiful, and luminous. In 1926 she founded the Civic Repertory Theatre, an enterprise that she maintained for nearly eight years. During that time she produced, directed, and acted in over thirty plays.

She has adopted as her own the White Chess Queen's line from her three productions (1932, 1947, 1982) of *Alice in Wonderland:* "Why, sometimes, I've believed as many as six impossible things before breakfast!"

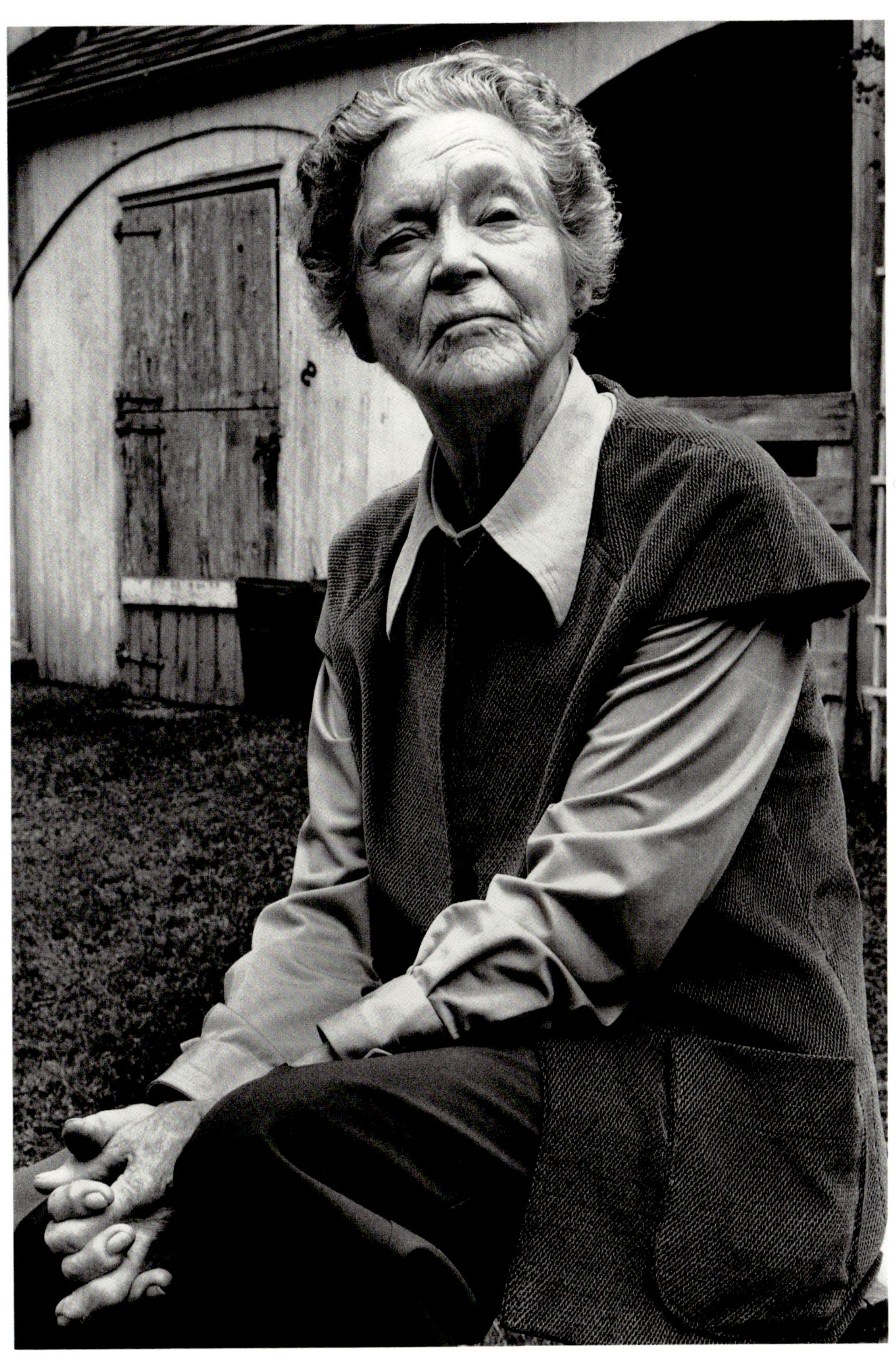

Malcolm Cowley

August 24, 1898

"The torture of my life," Malcolm Cowley has said, "is writing." Yet for over six decades this astute literary critic, author, and editor—who prefers to be called a literary historian—has continued to write. Since his eightieth birthday, three new books by Cowley have been published, including *The View from 80*—his thoughts on growing old. "To enter the country of age is a new experience," Cowley says, "different from what you supposed it to be. Nobody, man or woman, knows the country until he has lived in it and has taken out his citizenship papers. . . ."

Cowley was a member of the Lost Generation, that lively group of writers who lived and worked in Paris and in New York's Greenwich Village during the tumultuous decade following World War I. His most famous book, *Exile's Return,* records the intellectual odyssey of the writers of the 1920s.

In the sixty years since then Cowley has written and edited nearly a score of books. Everywhere in the converted Connecticut barn in which he lives are photographs that span these years. He refers to them frequently with visitors as he discusses his favorite subject, American literary history.

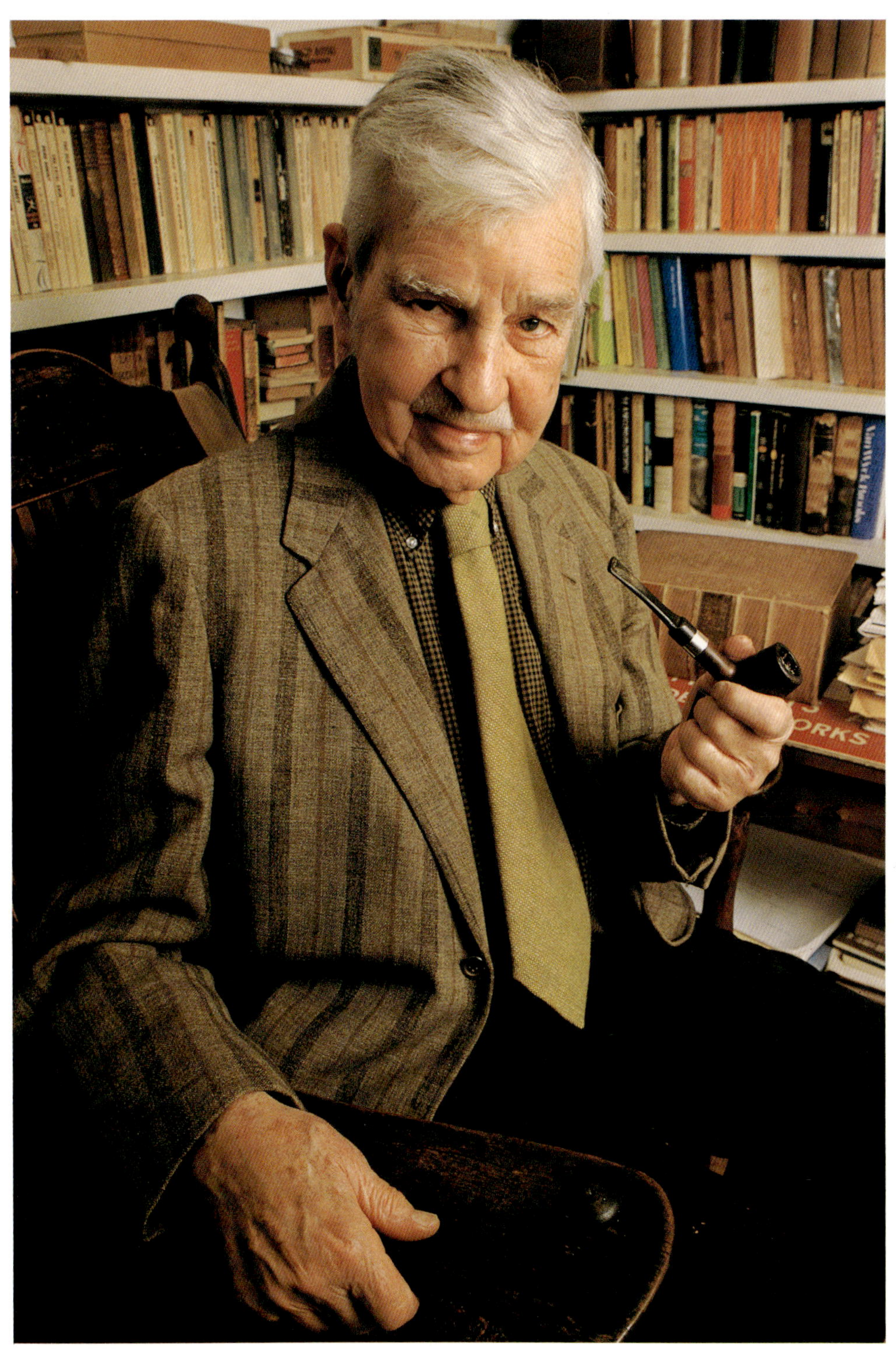

Linus Pauling

February 28, 1901

His two Nobel Prizes best define the major interests of Linus Pauling. After winning the Nobel Prize in Chemistry in 1954, he increasingly turned his attention to the effects of science on humanity. He never lacked the courage to take unpopular positions. He expounded the dangers of nuclear fallout and called for the end of nuclear weapons testing throughout the years of McCarthy and the Cold War, and in 1962 he was awarded the Nobel Peace Prize.

Pauling's scientific papers, books, academic appointments, honorary degrees, and awards are imposing in number. His scientific contributions have ranged from theories of chemical bonding to his popular work *Vitamin C and the Common Cold.*

Linus Pauling continues to be involved in scientific research and antinuclear activities. Unaccustomed to remaining still for any length of time, he begged me to hurry so that he could dash off to a nearby antinuclear demonstration.

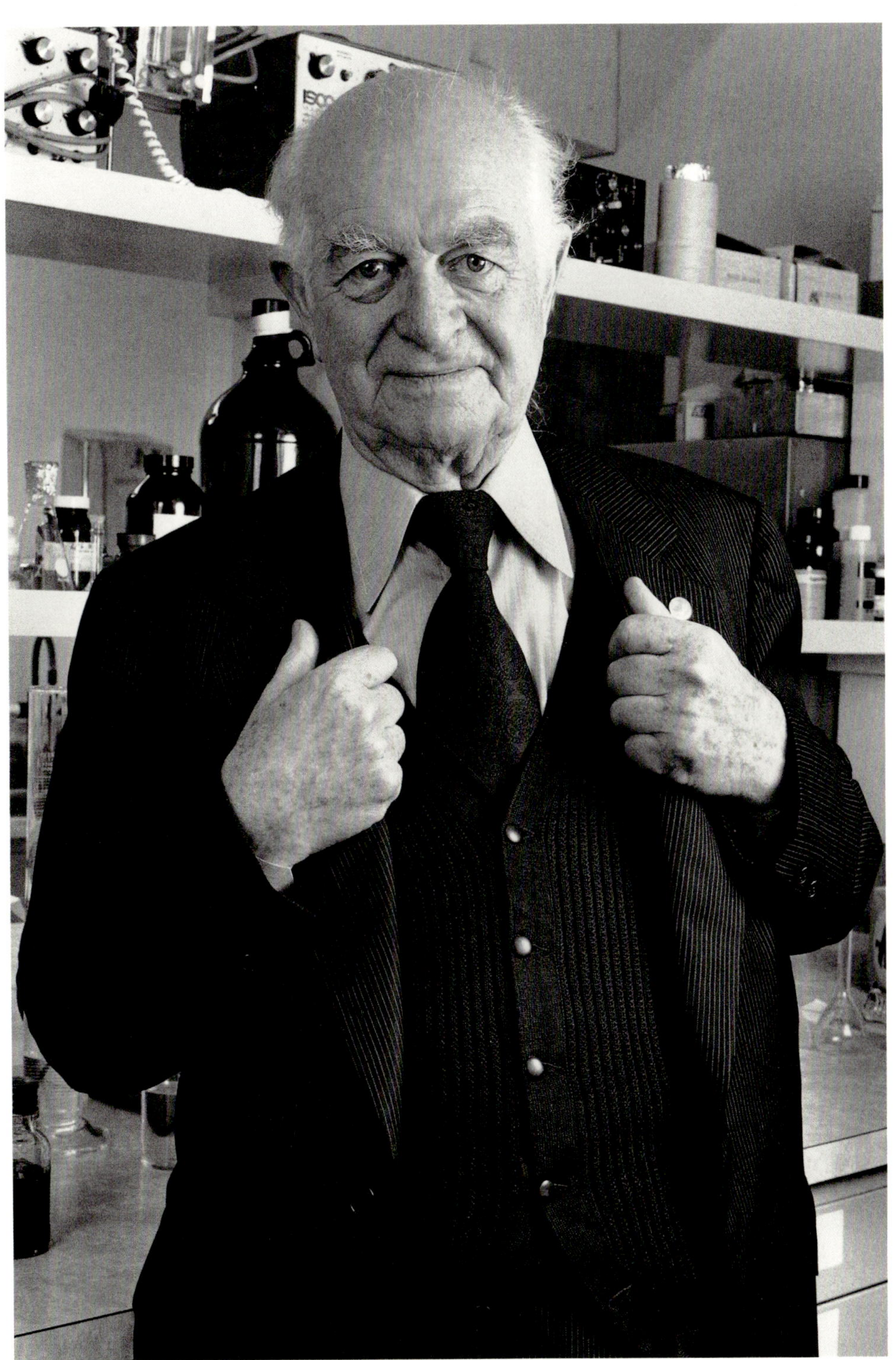

Louise Nevelson

September 23, 1900

Louise Nevelson told me she always knew she would be famous. While wide recognition did not come until she had reached her fifties, she is today regarded as one of the major and most original artists on the American scene.

Born in Kiev, Russia, Louise came to Maine with her family when she was five. She moved to New York in 1920, and by the early thirties began exhibiting her work. By the mid-1950s the artist and her environmental sculpture had achieved critical fame, and ever since her work has been exhibited in museums and galleries throughout the United States and Europe.

Louise Nevelson dresses in striking, unconventional clothes and flaunts eyelashes that have since become her trademark. An interviewer once asked her how she had chosen art as her career. With characteristic self-assurance Louise Nevelson replied, "I was born an artist."

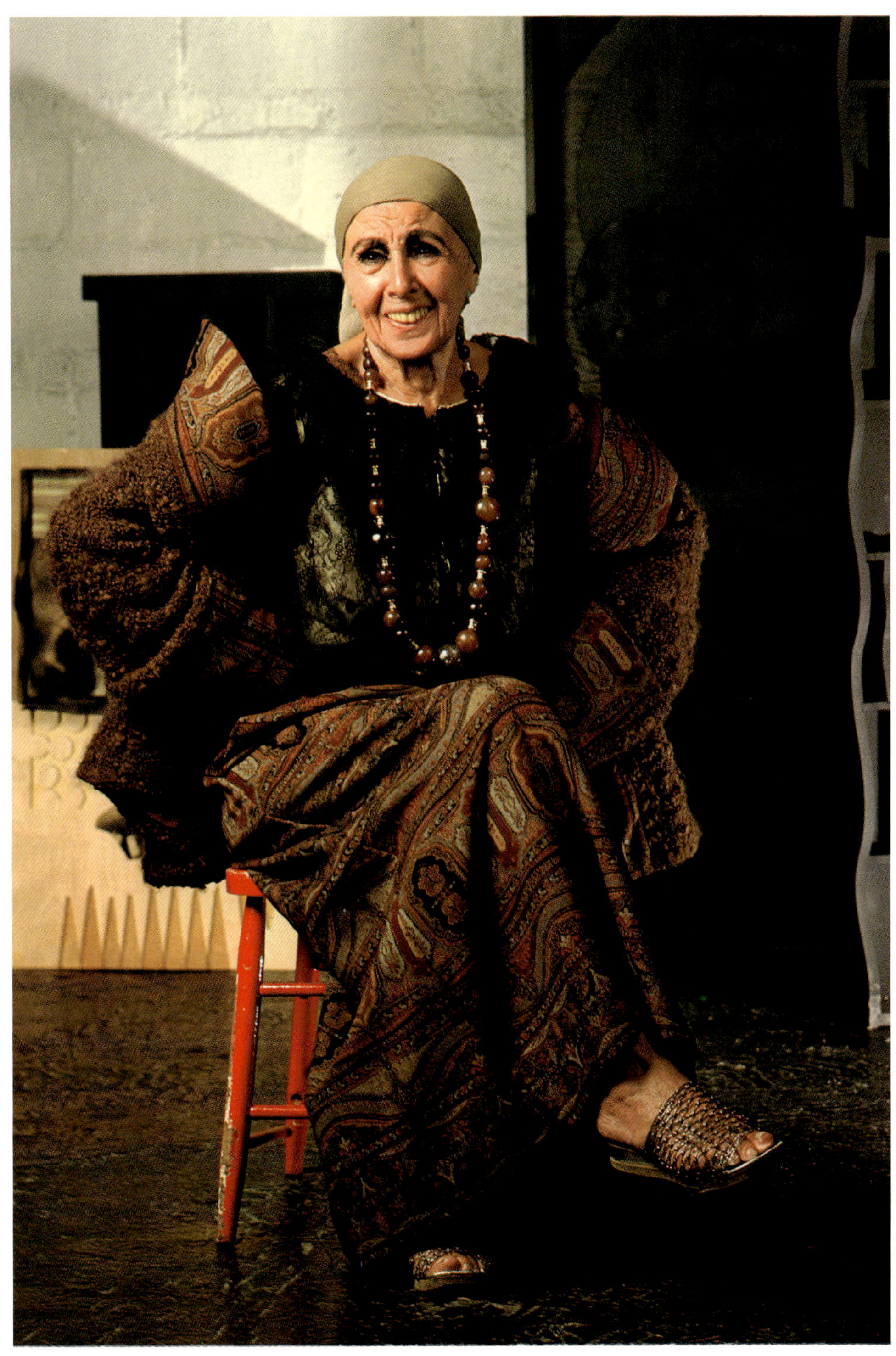

I. I. Rabi

July 29, 1898

Acknowledged as one of the outstanding atomic physicists of the twentieth century, Dr. I. I. Rabi usually accepts his countless honors with a large dose of self-irony. But when he received the Nobel Prize in 1944, he confided, he celebrated for six months.

In the years since, as an adviser to the United States government and the United Nations, he has turned his attention to controlling the dangers of nuclear energy.

Born in Austria-Hungary, Rabi was brought to Brooklyn, New York, as a child. Since 1923 he has been associated with Columbia University, where, as university professor emeritus, he continues to work. Since he no longer receives a salary, Rabi claims to be retired, adding with a smile, "Only poets never retire."

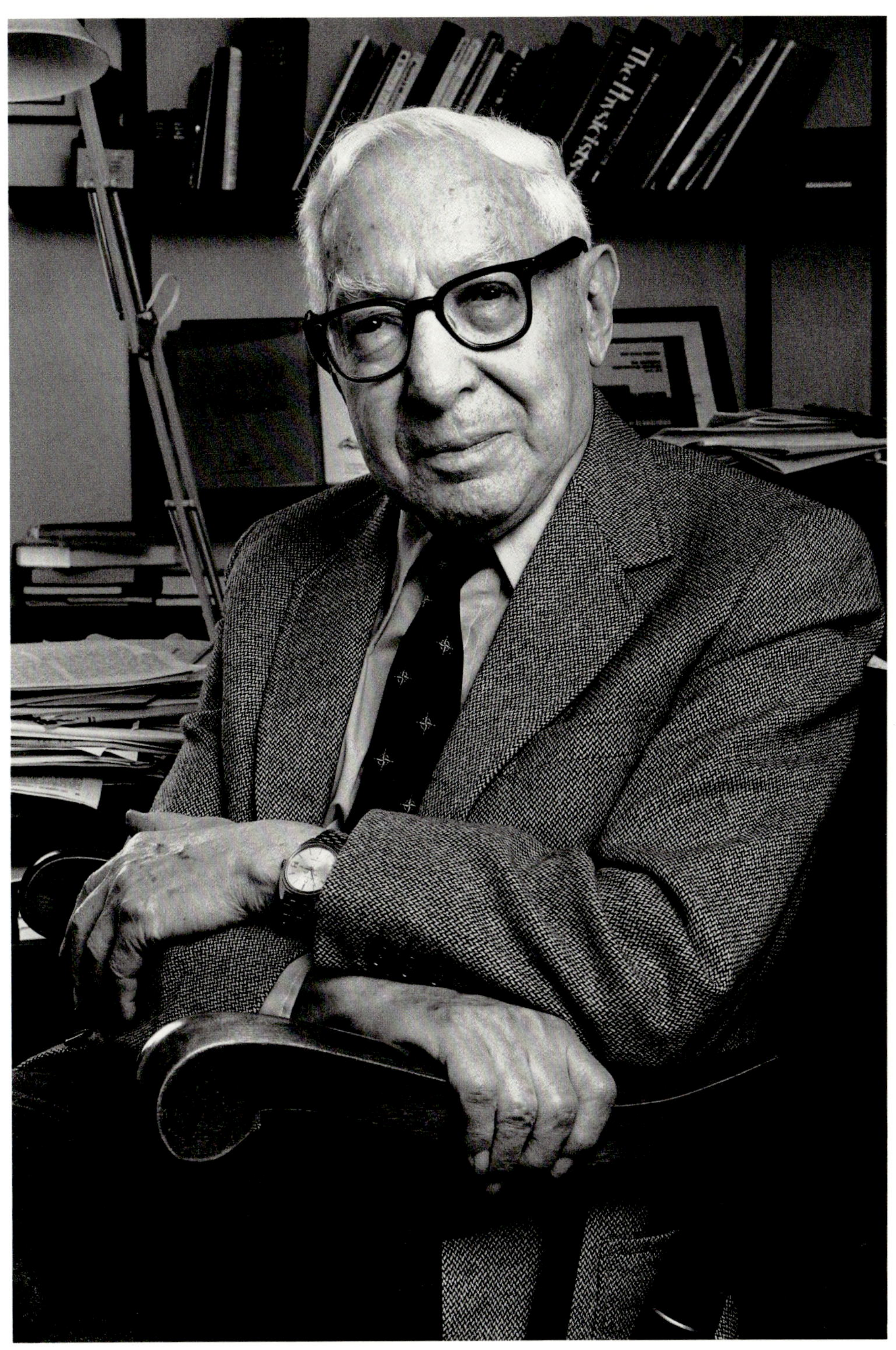
The Physicists

Louis Nizer

February 6, 1902

A best-selling author—*My Life in Court, The Jury Returns,* and others—who also paints and writes song lyrics, Louis Nizer is first and foremost a lawyer. He is a senior partner in a huge New York law firm and a noted authority on contracts, copyright law, and libel. In this last category he is known for having won the largest settlement to that date in a libel case he handled in behalf of World War II correspondent Quentin Reynolds.

Born in London, Nizer was brought to the United States by his parents at the age of three and grew up in Brooklyn. After graduating from Columbia University Law School, he entered private practice in New York City, where he has long represented the motion-picture industry and scores of famous actors, actresses, and authors.

Known for his eloquent and often brilliant presentations in court, Nizer maintains that they are the result of hard work, long hours, and sleepless nights. Once he was asked if there is such a thing as luck in trial law. "Yes," he replied, "but it only comes in the library at three o'clock in the morning."

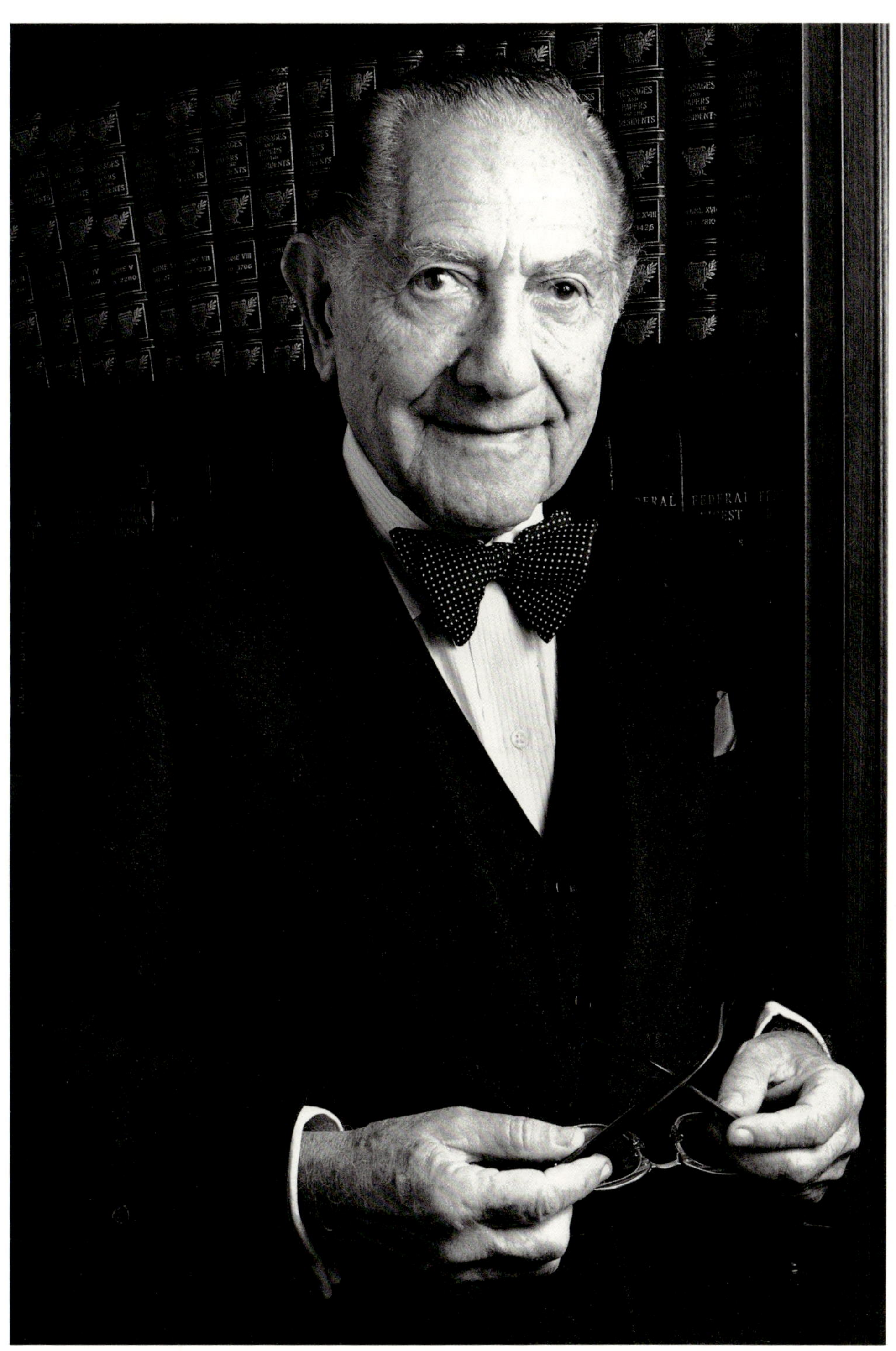

Barbara Morgan

July 8, 1900

At her husband Willard's urging, Barbara Morgan took up photography seriously in the early 1930s to illustrate the articles he wrote. She was a painter and teacher of art and design and found herself frustrated with the limitations of photography. She drew on her art background, experimenting with light, double images, photomontage.

The 1949 publication of *Martha Graham: Sixteen Dances in Photographs*—which she photographed, wrote, and designed—established her as one of the nation's outstanding and innovative photographers.

Barbara grew up in a close family. She has fond childhood memories of long philosophical conversations with her father. It is to her father's vivid descriptions of atoms "dancing" about in inanimate objects that she attributes her fascination with movement—clearly evidenced in her photographs of dance.

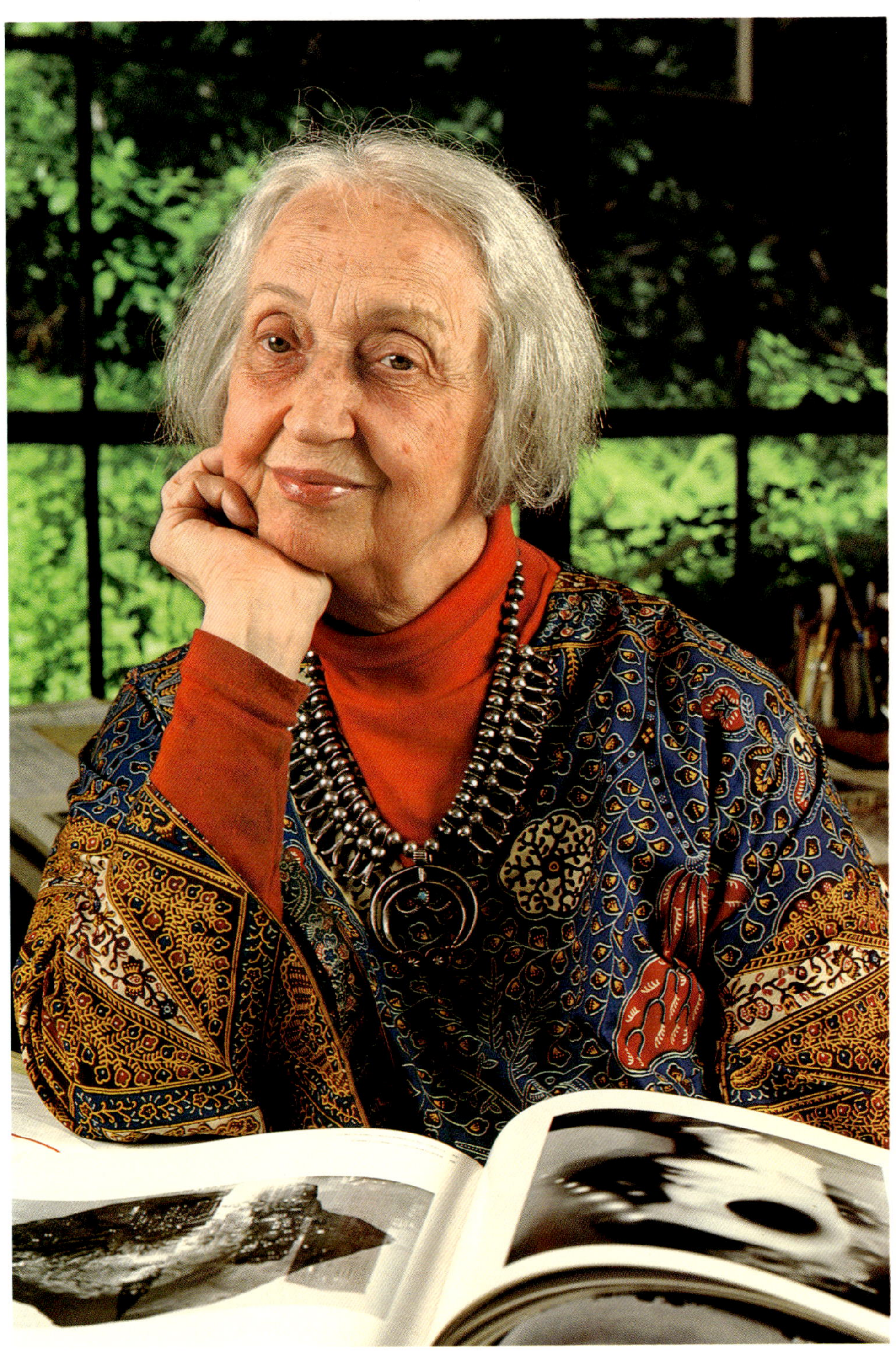

John Houseman

September 22, 1902

For John Houseman, the stock market crash of 1929 was the proverbial blessing in disguise. Forced to abandon his grain business, he embarked on a theatrical career as a producer, director, actor, and teacher.

He has worked with a number of famous theater groups, including Orson Welles's Mercury Theater and, most recently, the Acting Company, of which he is founder and artistic director.

Houseman has been the producer of many memorable films, among them *The Blue Dahlia, The Bad and the Beautiful, Julius Caesar,* and *They All Fall Down.* At the age of sixty-two he made his screen-acting debut, and at the age of seventy-one he won an Oscar for his role in *The Paper Chase.*

Recently in New York City for his duties with the Acting Company, he agreed to be photographed in Lincoln Center. Our photo session was delayed when a group of schoolchildren besieged Houseman with requests for autographs. It is ironic, he and I agreed, that after his many years in theater and film, he is more often recognized because of his TV commercials.

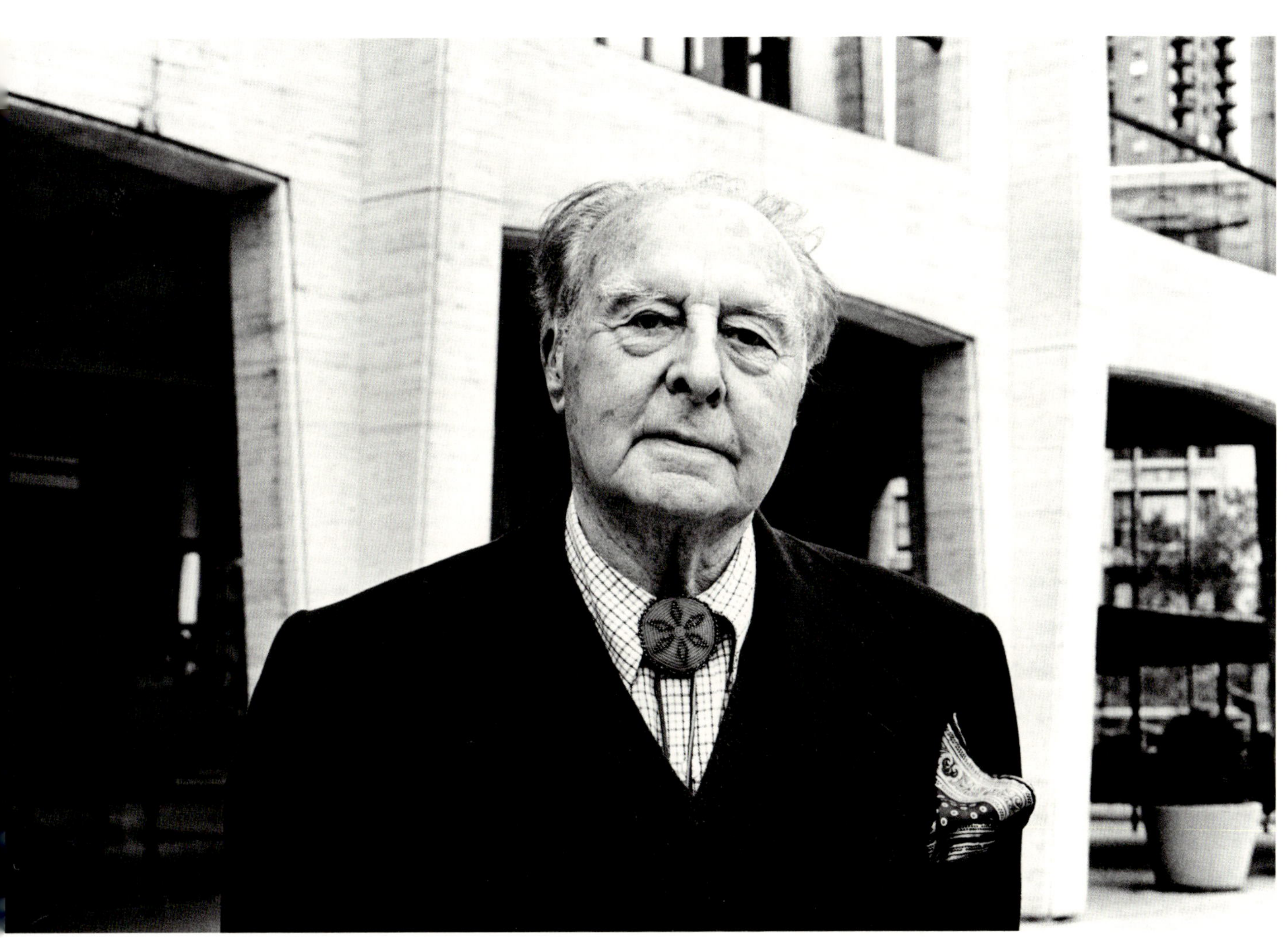

Otto Luening

June 15, 1900

Otto Luening is one of the most genuinely friendly and accepting men I have ever met. The openness that has made him a beloved teacher is immediately apparent in both his conversation and warm smile.

Luening's fame as a pioneer of electronic music has often obscured the vast body of more conservative work—more than three hundred pieces—he has composed for conventional instruments. He is an accomplished flutist and conductor as well. He retired from Columbia University in 1968—to a full schedule of composing, lecturing, and teaching. *The Odyssey of an American Composer,* his recent autobiography, chronicles his life and friendships through a half-century of American music.

Otto Luening offers this advice to any young artist: "Don't die young; don't take no for an answer—but don't be a fool!"

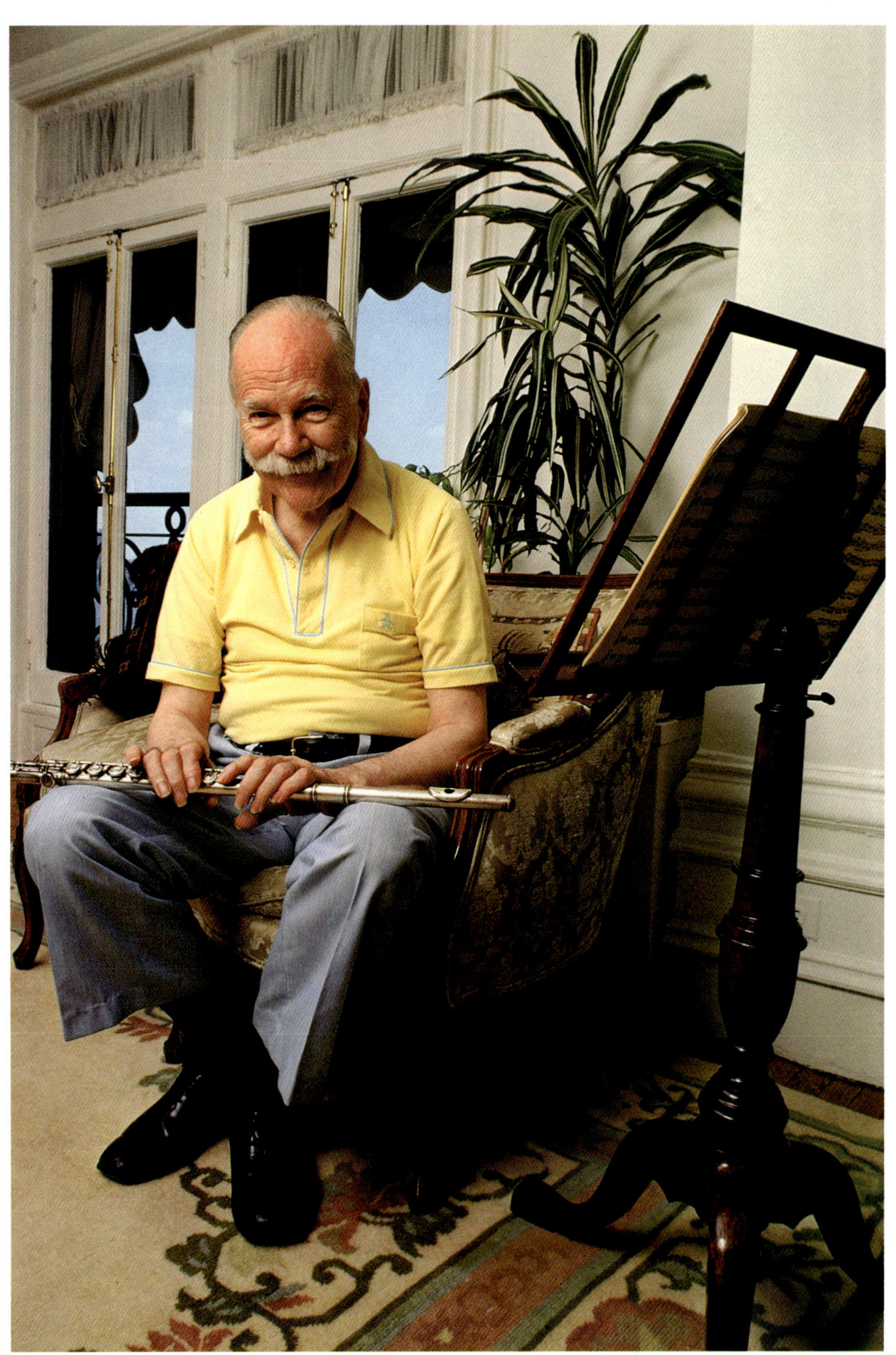

Joseph Buloff

December 6, 1899

Mention a country," says Joseph Buloff, "and I'll tell you what plays I did there." It is scarcely an exaggeration. Buloff started out with the famed Vilna Troupe in Lithuania in the years immediately following the First World War, and has since performed in Yiddish and English throughout the world—in Europe, Latin America, Israel, South Africa, the United States.

"I've appeared in 226 plays. I've played so many parts, I don't know who I am," he said. But the American public knows him as the peddler in the original *Oklahoma!* and for his role in the play *The Price.* He has just completed a Broadway run and is awaiting the next call.

Joe Buloff, with his resonant voice and trace of an accent, reminds me of an Old World Jewish philosopher. "What can I say about myself?" he asked. "I've had a lot of aggravation, a lot of joy—a lot of life!"

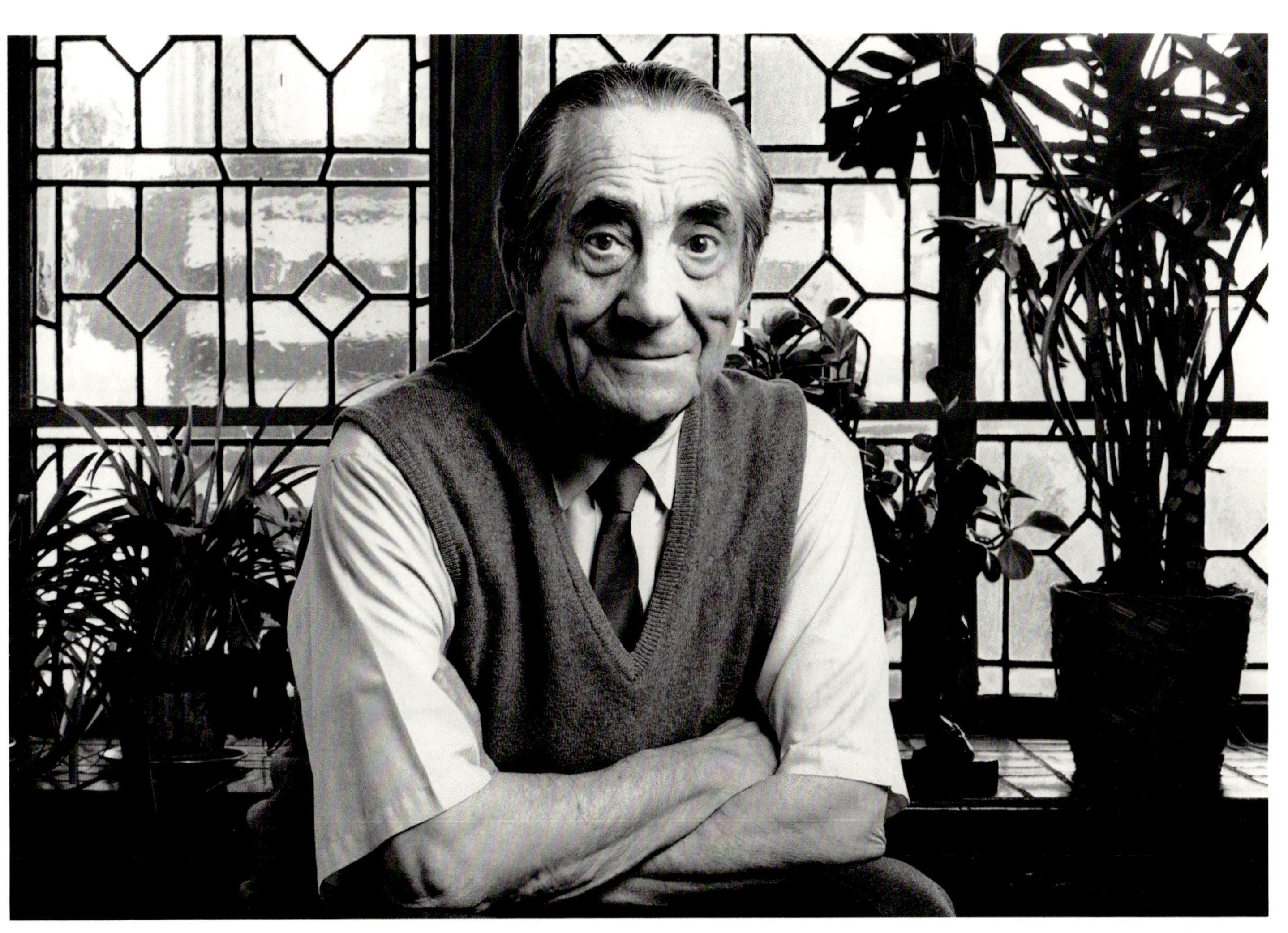

Virgil Thomson

November 25, 1896

Diverse" is the word most often used to characterize Virgil Thomson's abilities. He has composed symphonies, concertos, sonatas, ballets, and background music for theater. His music for the 1948 *Louisiana Story* won the only Pulitzer Prize ever awarded a film score. He won popular recognition as well as critical acclaim for two operas with librettos by Gertrude Stein—*Four Saints in Three Acts* and *The Mother of Us All.*

The pungent, perceptive, and often provocative pieces he wrote as music critic for the New York *Herald Tribune* from 1940 to 1954 established him as a major critical writer.

Also famous—or perhaps infamous—for his proclivity for falling asleep everywhere and anywhere, Virgil Thomson lived up to his reputation—briefly dozing while I changed the film in my camera.

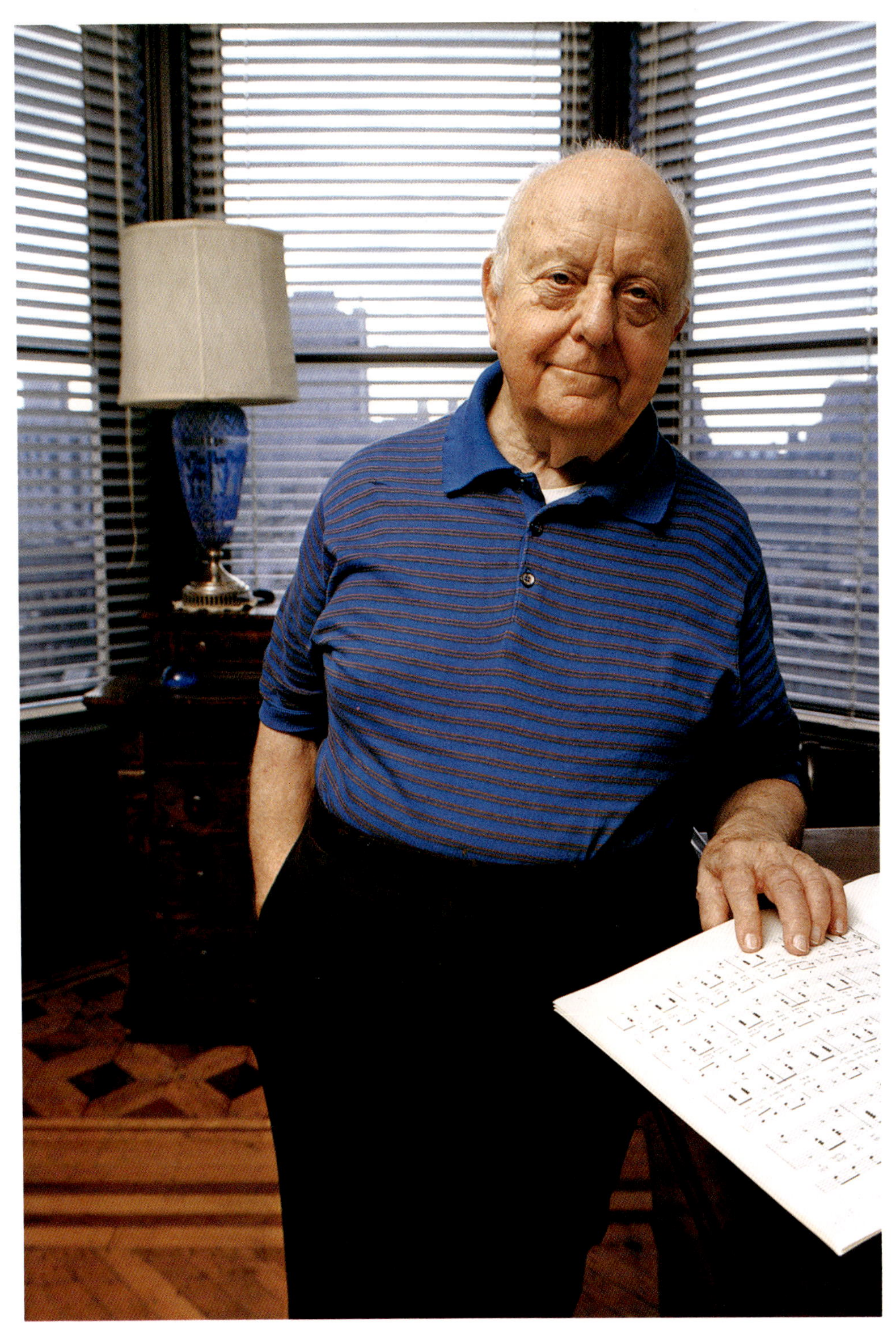

Armand Hammer

May 21, 1898

Armand Hammer has never lost his Midas touch. Chairman of Occidental Petroleum and owner of a variety of enterprises, including two art galleries, he is constantly embarking on the flamboyant—and always highly profitable—deals that are his trademark.

A nonpracticing physician, Dr. Hammer made his first million dollars while still in medical school. He went to Moscow in 1921 to aid the typhus-stricken Russian people in the aftermath of the First World War. However, his business acumen proved more valuable than his medical skills, and Hammer was soon putting together imaginative deals between the young Soviet government and American firms. He left Moscow nine years later with his fortune made—and a priceless collection of Russian art.

Single-minded concentration must be one key to Hammer's success. While I photographed him, he remained totally absorbed in a tape recording of a business interview, and neither responded to my questions nor uttered one word.

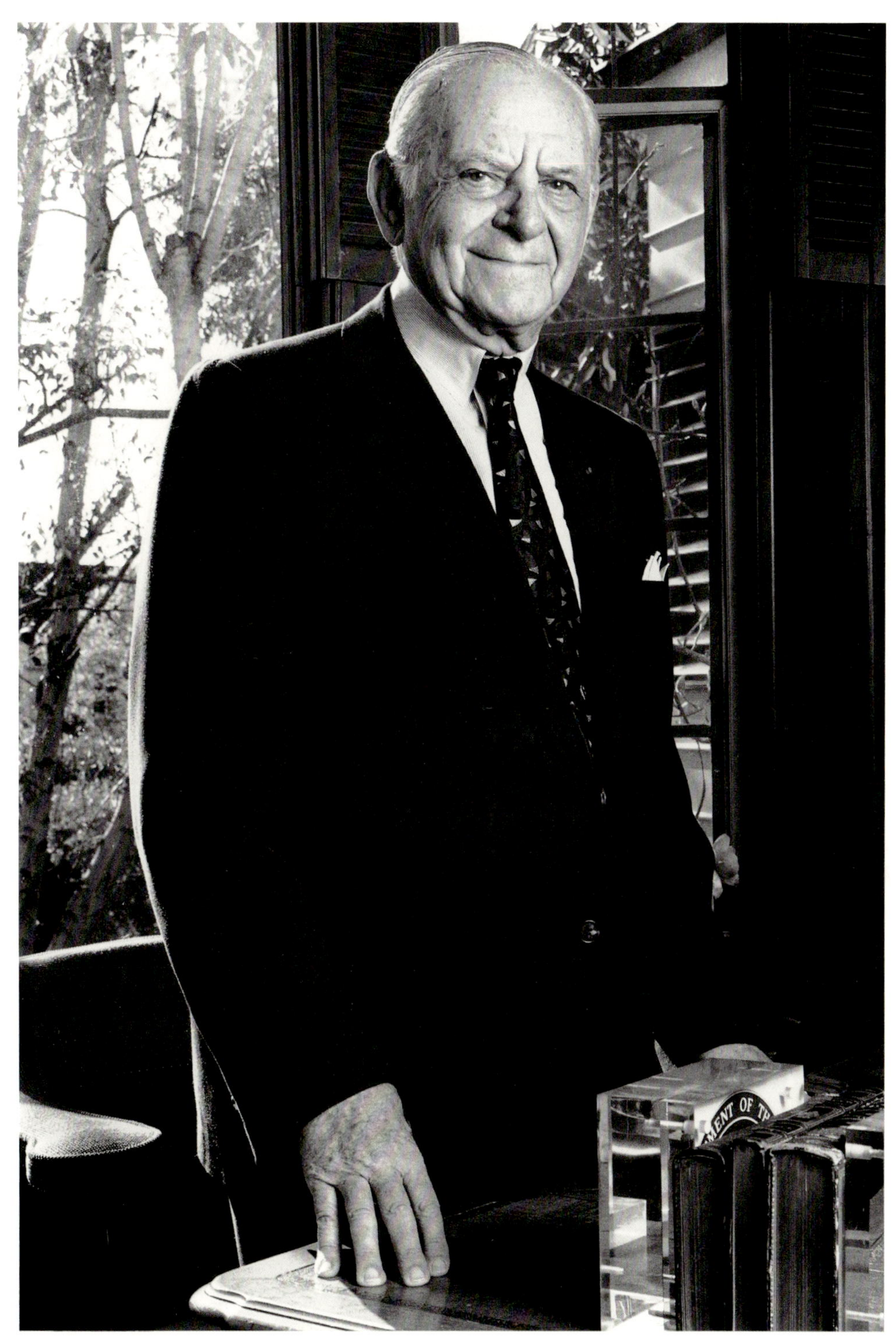

Samson Raphaelson

March 30, 1896

To be a writer, Samson Raphaelson told me, you must have both passion and pain. His own writing grew out of his pain at being "a skinny guy with glasses who could never be football captain or two-step champion." And his passion—"the ability to sit at a typewriter for three hours or three days, staring at one paragraph, knowing you can make it work"—has not dimmed with the years.

Both a playwright and Hollywood writer, Rafe calls the theater "my one true love." He has written nine Broadway plays, among them *The Jazz Singer, Accent on Youth,* and *Skylark.* Rafe's screen credits include *Trouble in Paradise, The Shop Around the Corner,* and the original *Heaven Can Wait.*

Passion is the word I will always associate with Rafe. Now in his eighth year of teaching in the theater and film departments of Columbia University, he is still sharing the savvy of half a century of writing—his passion for the craft he calls "the sheer awareness of life and the talent to use that awareness."

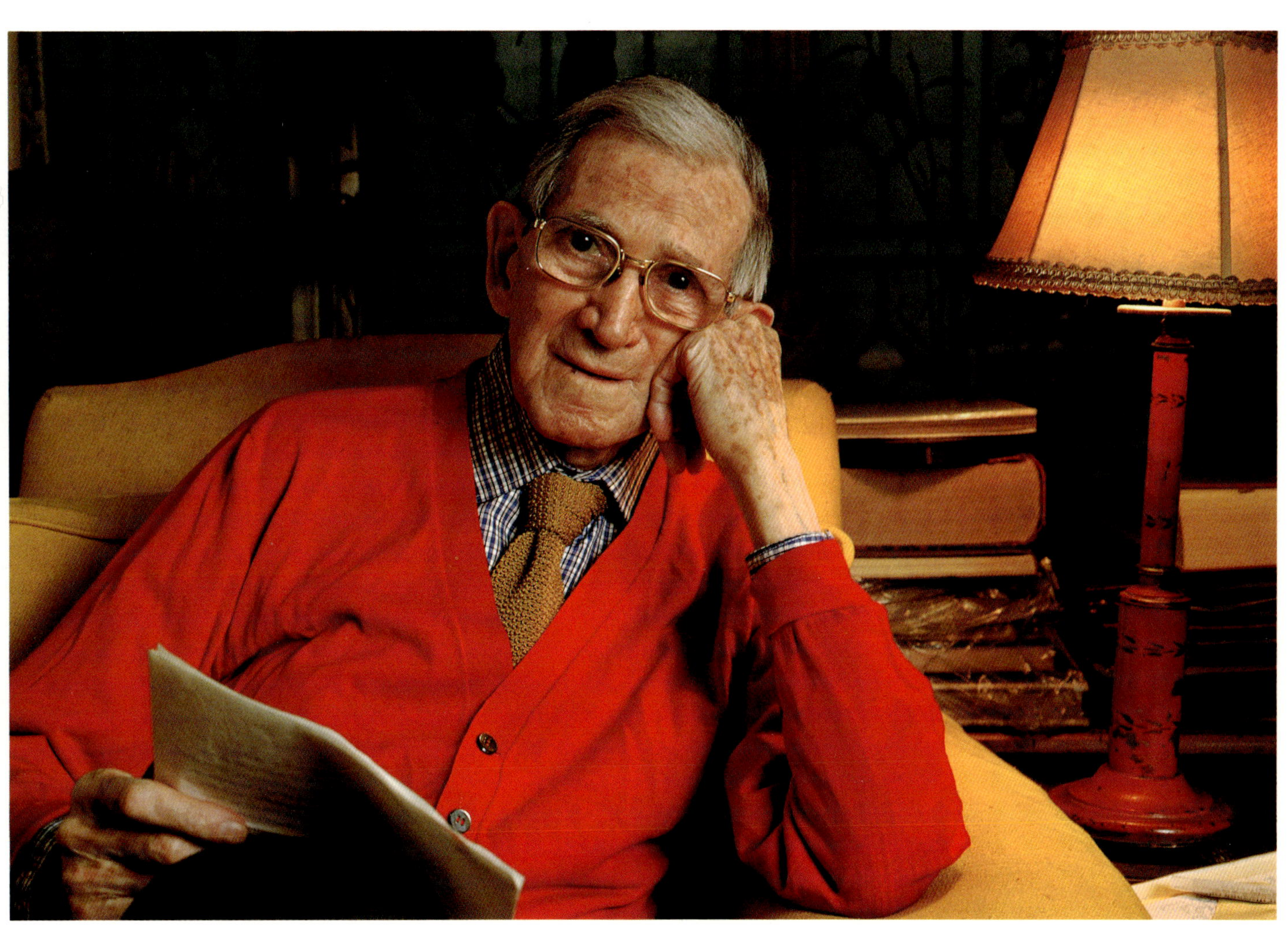

Raphael Soyer

December 25, 1899

Raphael Soyer inspired this book. Since 1973, when I first modeled for him, he has been my friend.

For Raphael life and work are synonymous. The people and streets of New York City are his world. When he travels, he knows he has been away too long if a certain dream of being locked out of his studio recurs.

While the faces of family and friends appear time and again through his sixty years of paintings and drawings, there is one clearly recognizable face that always pops up—often hovering in the background or at the edge of a crowd—his own.

Recognition is his. His self-portrait hangs in the Uffizi Gallery in Florence—an honor shared by few other Americans. But neither renown nor age has changed his attitudes. He befriends all—but reserves for the young a special place in his heart.

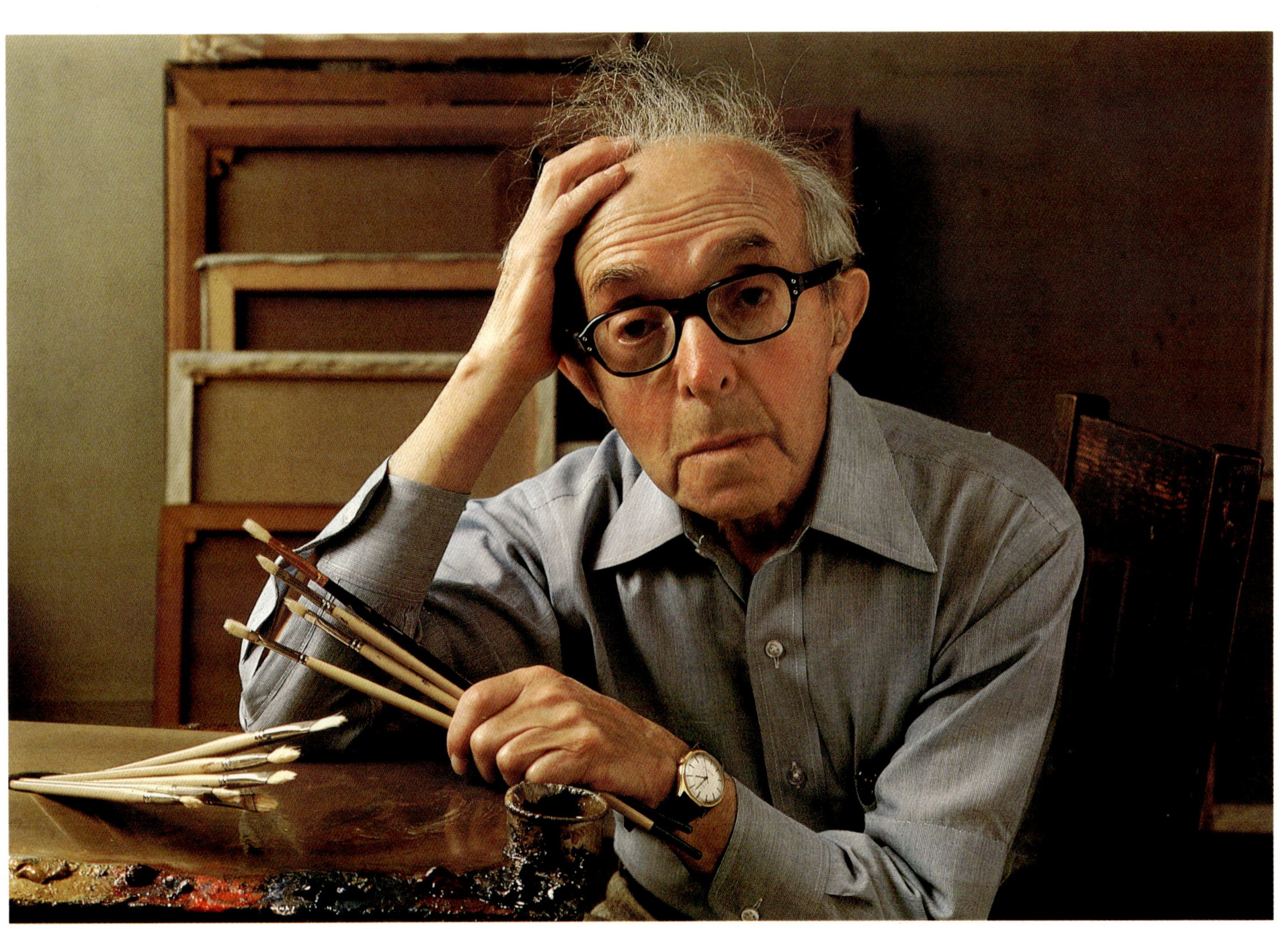

Glenway Wescott

April 11, 1901

Monroe Wheeler

February 3, 1901

Glenway Wescott and Monroe Wheeler share a midwestern upbringing, an interest in literature and art, and sixty years of friendship. They met at the University of Chicago, and shortly thereafter, Wheeler, who at the time was a publisher, brought out Wescott's first book.

During the 1920s, Wescott and Wheeler shared the life of the many literary and artistic Americans in France. They returned to the United States in 1934.

Wescott (seated on the left) has written novels, short stories, poetry, and criticism. Wheeler was director of exhibitions and publications at The Museum of Modern Art in New York City and is the author of several books on art.

Someone once asked them how two such cantankerous people have managed to spend so much time together for so many years. Wescott chuckled and replied, "We're never afraid to quarrel, and we have the energy to give."

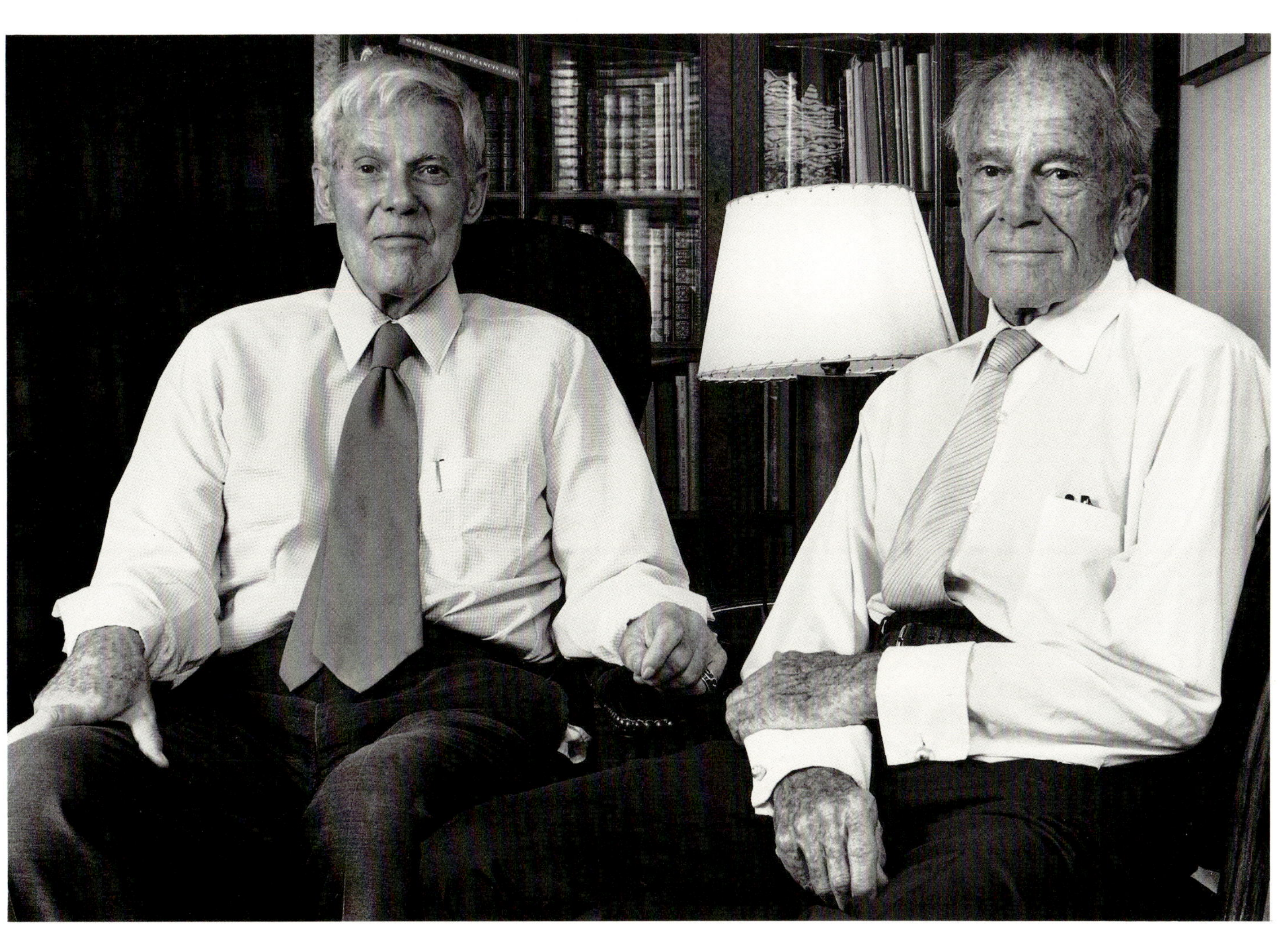

Abe Lastfogel

May 17, 1898

Abe Lastfogel was born the same year the William Morris Agency was founded, a significant fact since he was to become its president fifty-four years later. Lastfogel began his career at the agency as an office boy in 1912, when the staff numbered four.

In 1933, and the agency much grown, Lastfogel moved to the company's Los Angeles office as its vice president and set up housekeeping in the Beverly Wilshire Hotel, a place he has continued to live in ever since. During his years with William Morris (he is now chairman emeritus) Lastfogel was considered the top talent agent in the country and represented personalities as diverse as Elvis Presley and Sophia Loren. Today he maintains a Beverly Hills office, where he spends his mornings; in the afternoons he can be found screening the latest movies.

A. L., as he has become known in the industry, is a self-made man whose meteoric rise once prompted the humorist S. J. Perelman to proclaim: "Hollywood is . . . where the first fogel shall be Lastfogel."

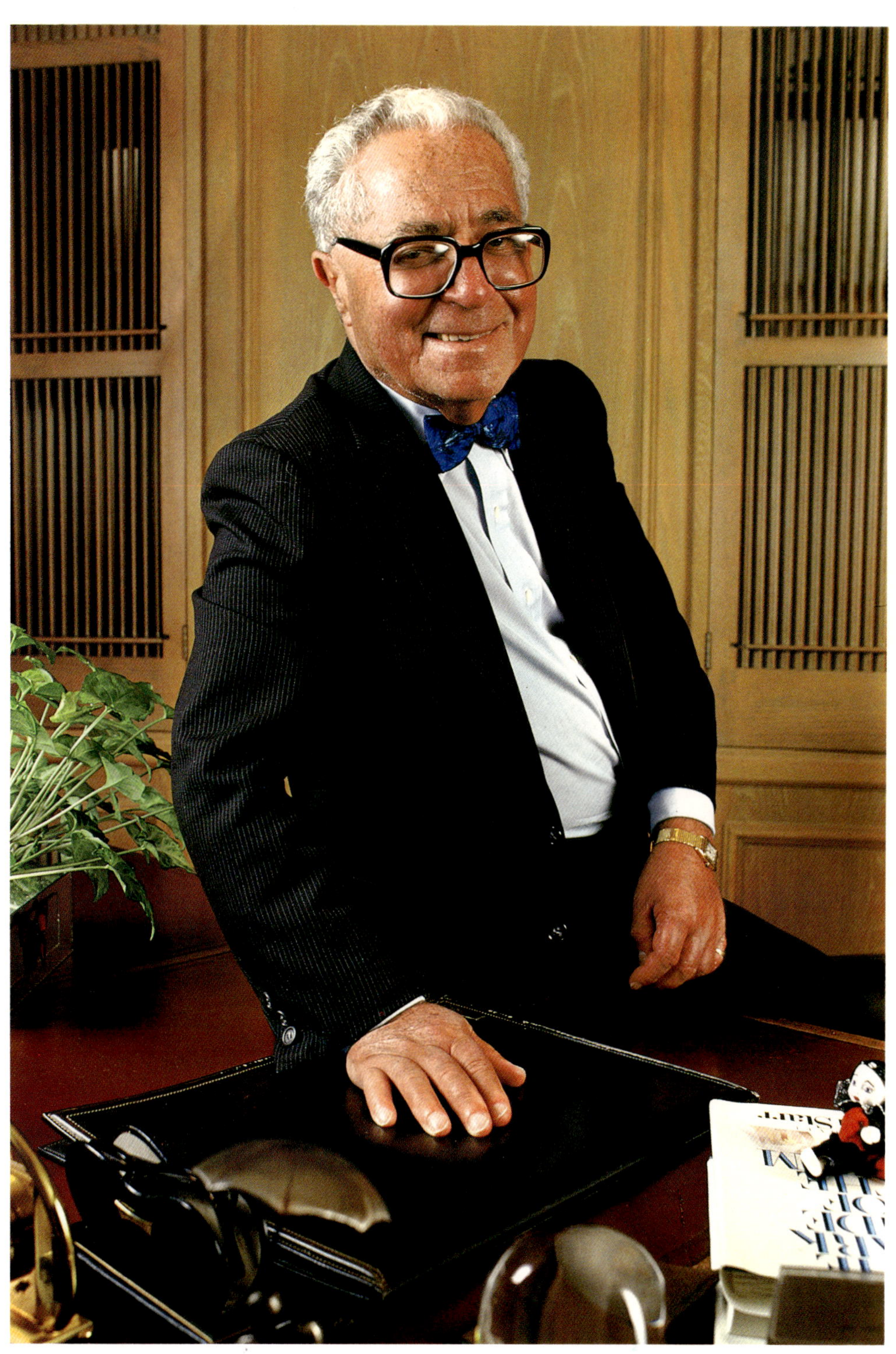

Rouben Mamoulian

October 8, 1898

Like many of the other octogenarians I have met, Rouben Mamoulian expressed surprise at finding himself in his eighties. "I don't know how I got here," he remarked. "I was always the youngest in my crowd."

Mamoulian's lyrical and impressionistic style of directing was indelibly stamped on such Broadway hits as *Porgy and Bess* and *Carousel.* Following his first film, *Applause,* in 1929, he commuted between Broadway and Hollywood. He is an independent, imaginative, and often witty film director, whose screen credits include *Becky Sharp, Dr. Jekyll and Mr. Hyde, Gay Desperado, The Mark of Zorro,* and *Silk Stockings.*

Sitting in front of a portrait of himself by his wife, Mamoulian spoke of his trademark—at least one cat in every film. But his favorite cat, Nefertiti, refused to sit still and pose for me.

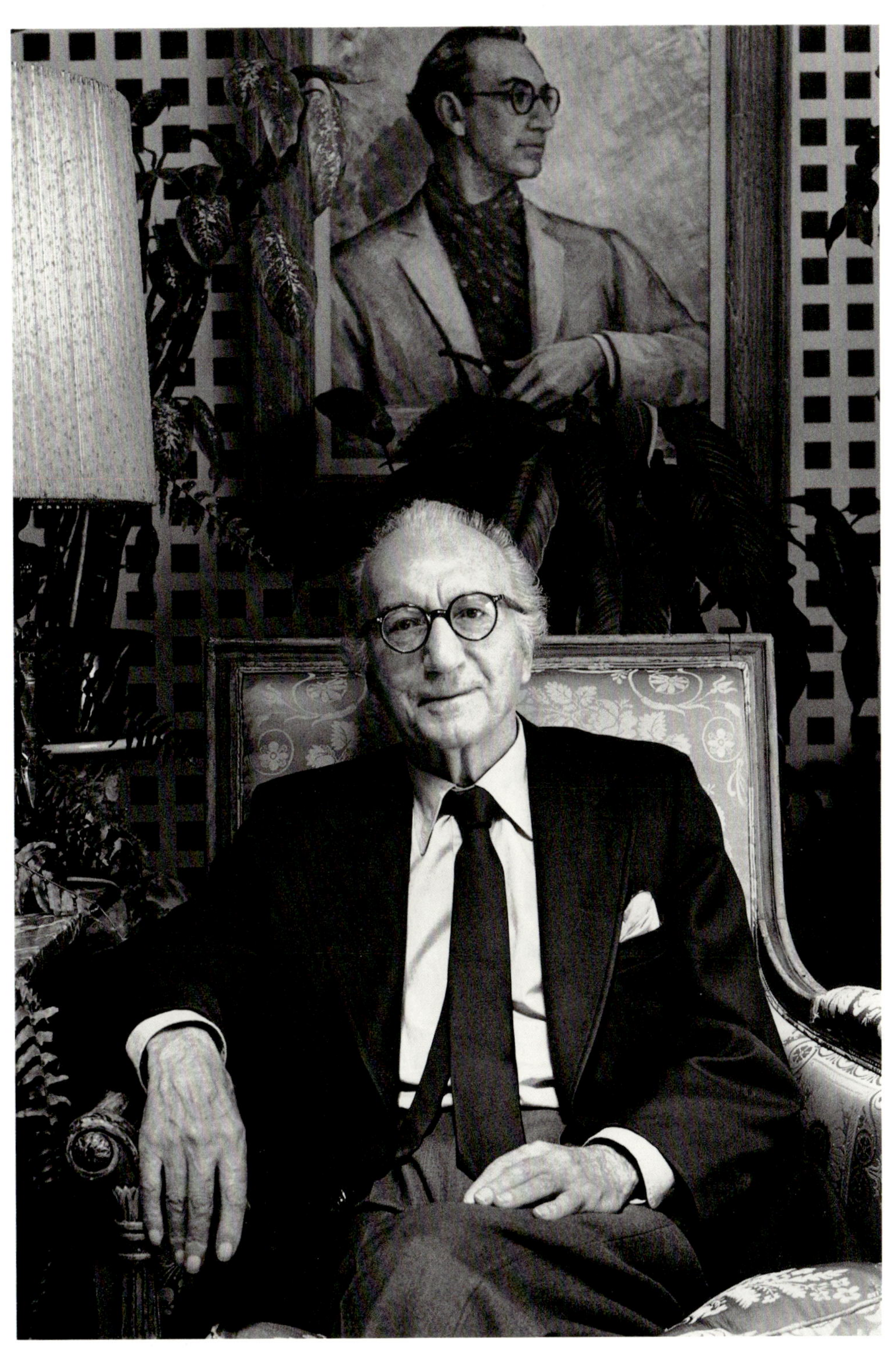

George Burns

January 20, 1896

Whether on TV or in the privacy of his Beverly Hills home, George Burns's jokes and patter are close to nonstop—delivered with impeccable timing around the ever-present cigar. Not certain how to address him, I asked if I might call him George. "Sure, you can call me George," came the reply, ". . . or you can call me Sam. . . ."

Born Nathan Birnbaum on New York's Lower East Side, he started entertaining at the age of fourteen. There followed years as a vaudeville performer in acts he describes as so awful he had to change his name after each booking. He was George Burns when, in 1923, he met an unemployed actress named Gracie Allen—and the Burns and Allen team was launched on five decades of unparalleled show business success.

A familiar face to tens of millions of television viewers, George has been performing alone for the past two decades since Gracie died. In 1976, at the age of eighty, he won an Oscar for his role in *The Sunshine Boys.*

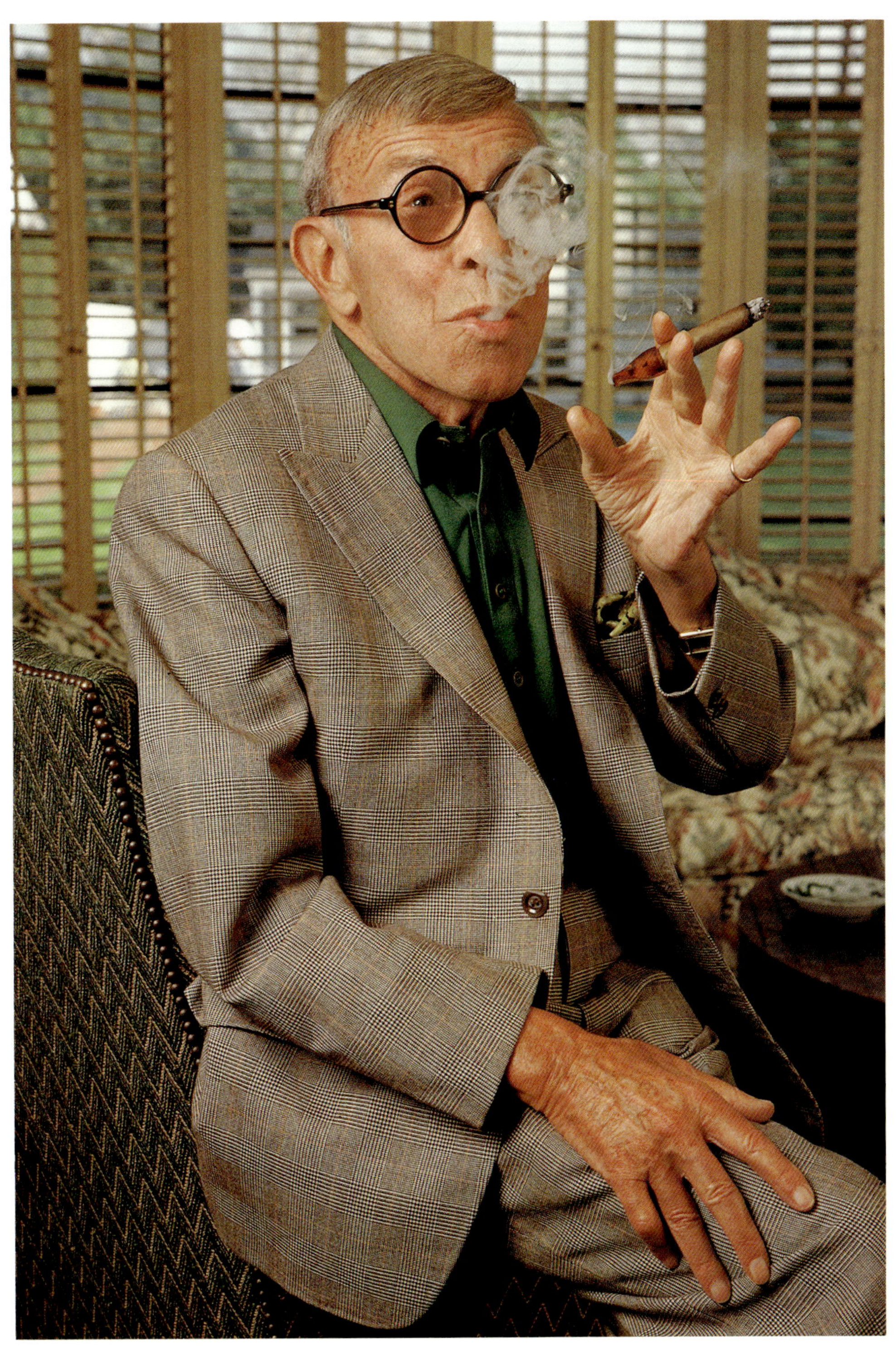

Molly Picon

February 28, 1898

Molly Picon made her theatrical debut on a Philadelphia trolley car at the age of five. A drunk asked the child why she was wearing fancy clothes. When Molly told him she was on her way to appear at a children's amateur night, he challenged her to perform on the spot. She belted out her song, and the drunk passed a hat, collecting five dollars from the other passengers in the car. Molly went on to win the five-dollar first prize at the amateur show—and brought home more money that night than her grandfather earned in a week.

It was the start of a career that is still going strong. A star of the Yiddish theater and a veteran vaudevillian, Molly is a performer on Broadway and television as well. She has acted, sung, and danced her way into the hearts of audiences throughout the United States, Europe, and Latin America.

Molly only stopped doing handstands onstage at eighty-one. "My doctor," she says with a laugh, "told me, 'Enough is enough!' " She loves to play the *schmendrick* (the Yiddish word for fool) and throughout the photo session this little lady kept mugging and crossing her eyes.

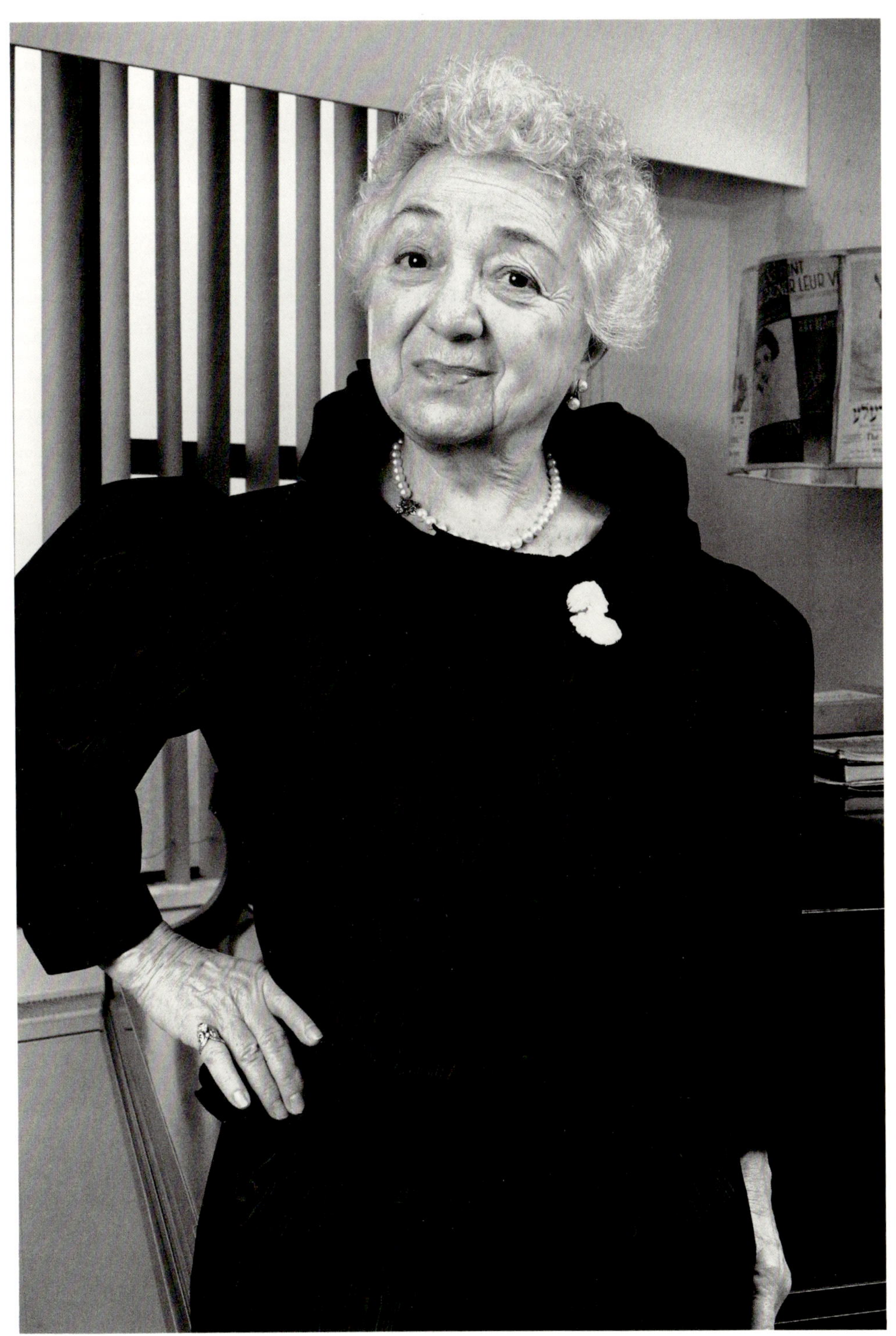

Norman Vincent Peale

May 31, 1898

Dr. Norman Vincent Peale is Mr. Positive Thinking. His boundless enthusiasm—and ability to communicate it effectively through TV and radio as well as in person—have made him one of the most influential clergymen in the United States.

This down-to-earth preacher is the author of twenty-nine books—among them *The Power of Positive Thinking,* one of the all-time best-sellers in America. With his upbeat message and dynamic delivery, Dr. Peale is in constant demand as a speaker at religious and business functions.

Minister of the Marble Collegiate Reformed Church in New York City, Dr. Peale, along with his wife, publishes *Guideposts,* a monthly magazine with a readership of thirteen million.

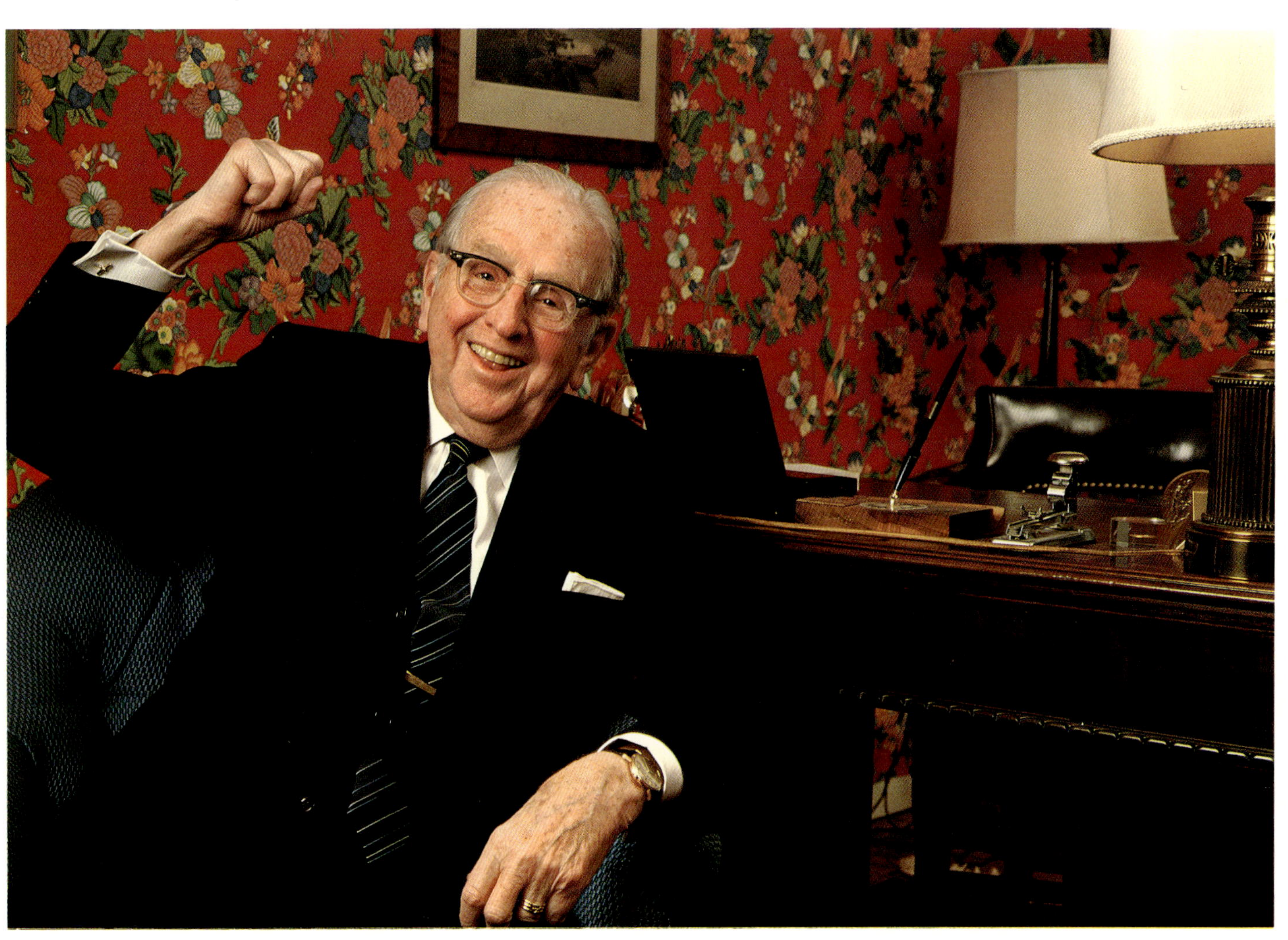

George S. Halas

February 2, 1895

"Papa Bear" is the father not only of the Chicago Bears but of professional football as well. In 1920, the year that George S. Halas formed the team that would soon become the Chicago Bears, he was one of a small group of men who organized the American Professional Football Association—the direct forerunner of the National Football League.

In addition to being the club's founder and president, Halas played end for the Bears throughout the 1920s, and for forty years served as the team's head coach. Halas's competitive drive and unswerving commitment to professional football have played a major role in winning the game its dominant place in American sports.

George Halas remains active as chief executive of the Bears. He credits his stamina to his outlook on aging: "I never had time to get old."

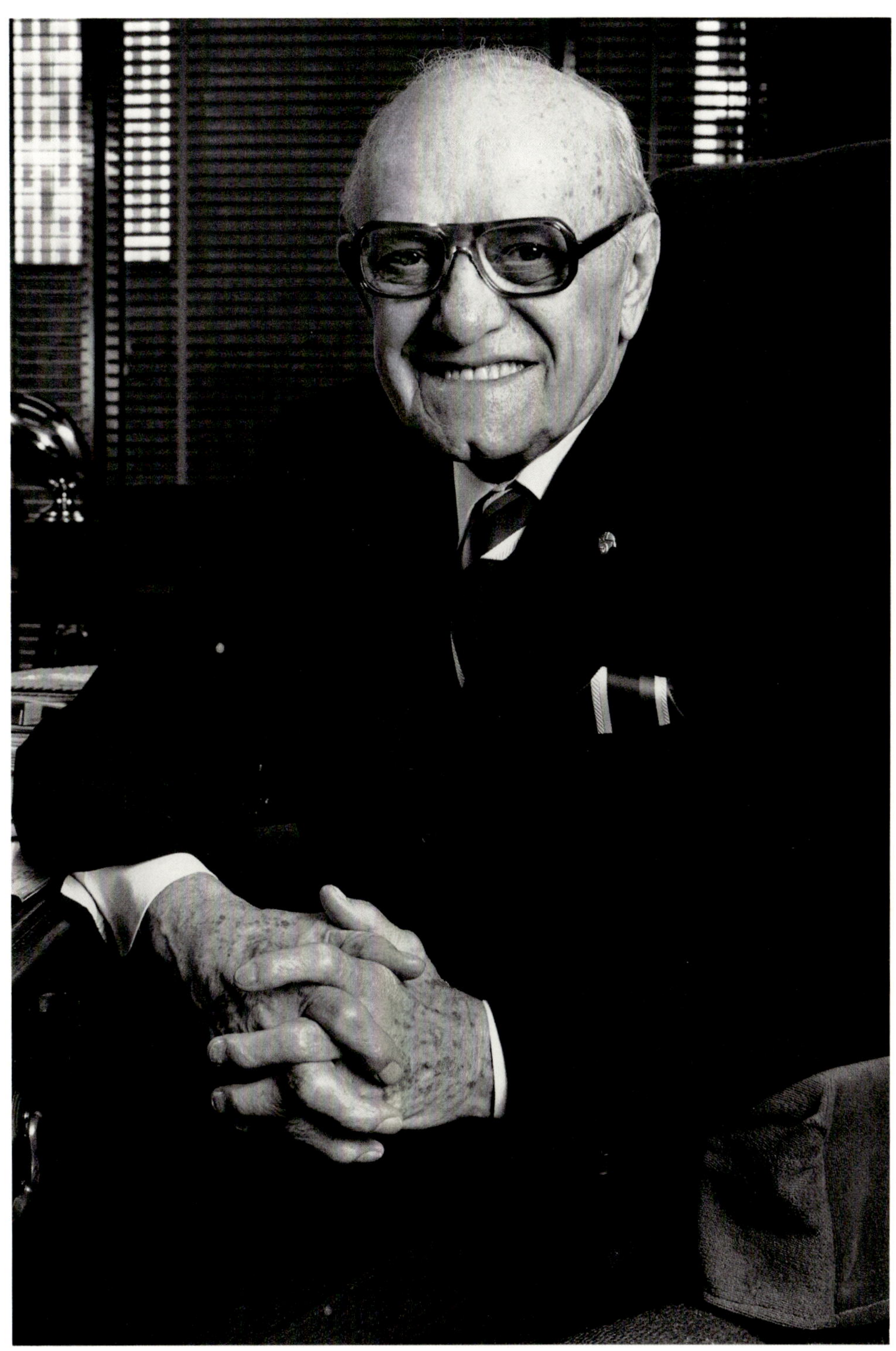

Isabel Bishop

March 3, 1902

Work is Isabel Bishop's greatest joy. Full of enthusiasm and energy, she commutes daily from her home in an outlying section of New York City to her studio on Union Square. While she makes the long trip by subway or bus, she often does quick sketches of her fellow passengers.

A native of Cincinnati, Ohio, Isabel came to New York in 1918 to study art, and she has made the city her home and subject ever since. An incredibly sweet and modest woman, she communicates her enduring passion for life and for art.

Isabel is happiest on Union Square, surrounded by the people she loves to observe and paint. The workers, students, shoppers, and bums who occupy the square fill her paintings and are always in motion, rendered like the stopped-action shots of early pre-motion-picture photography. It is her special way of expressing the vitality she sees in all members of the human race.

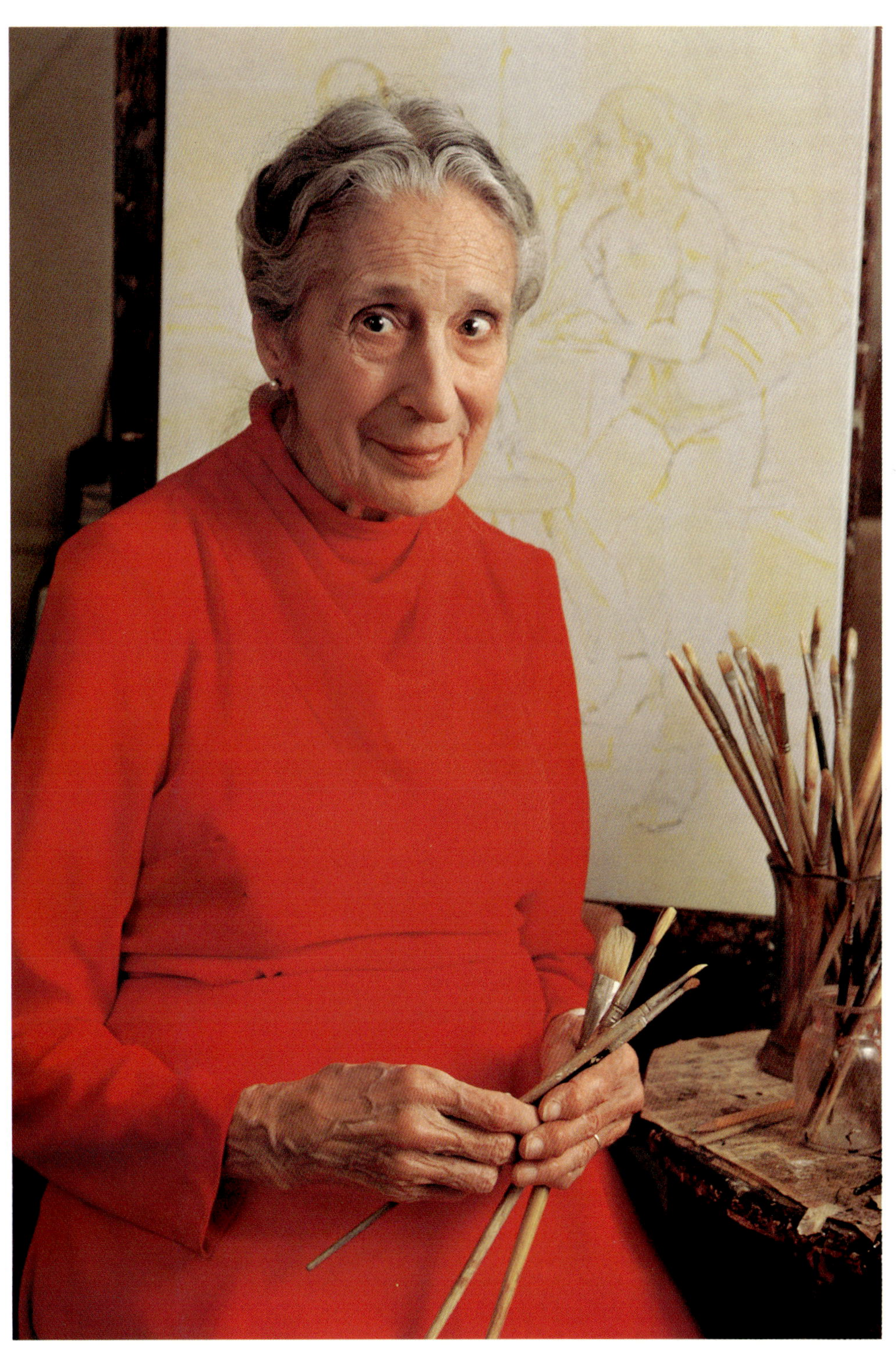

Sam J. Ervin, Jr.

September 27, 1896

Despite his claim to be just an "old country lawyer," Sam Ervin has been a national figure since 1973, when he was chairman of the Senate committee investigating the abuses of presidential power under Richard Nixon. The committee's televised Watergate hearings made an overnight hero of the courtly Democrat from North Carolina, who, with his biblical quotations and down-home wisdom, reassured the American people that not all Washington was cowed by the power of the president.

"If the American people will take care of the Constitution, it will take care of them," Sam Ervin told me. His staunch commitment to his interpretation of the rights and safeguards provided by the United States Constitution is the common thread running through his twenty years in the United States Senate.

At the end of 1974, Senator Sam "retired" to Morganton, North Carolina, where on his eighty-sixth birthday he completed his autobiography. He maintains that since he was born not three hundred feet from where he now lives, he never really went very far.

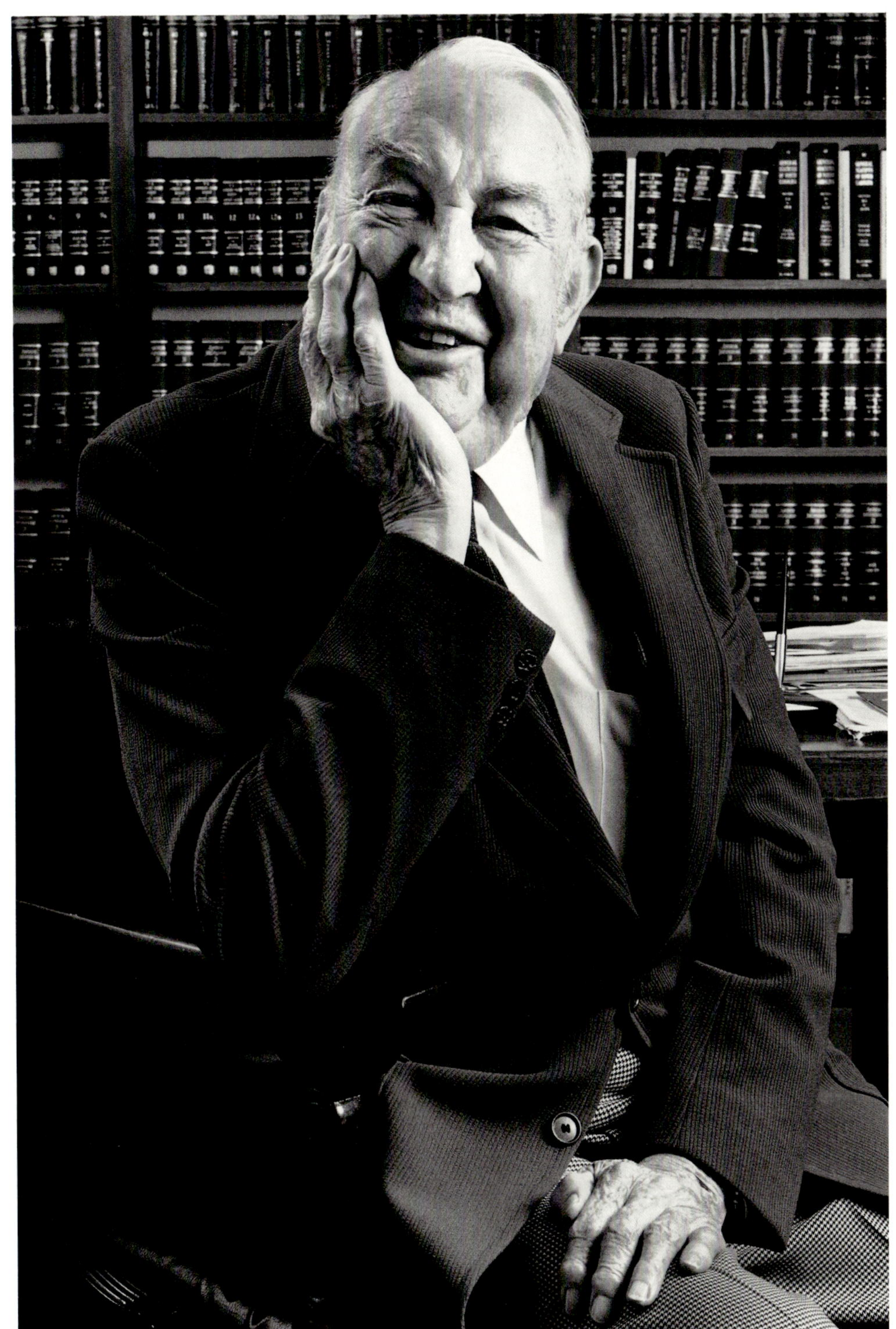

Sippie Wallace

November 1, 1898

Houston-born Sippie Wallace, singer and writer of the blues, is known for her sassy style and strong lyrics. By the age of seven, Sippie was singing in the church choir and playing the piano. At ten she was sneaking out of the house to sing the blues and was soon performing in the Houston tent shows—the only theater available to blacks at the time.

Between 1923—when she made her first recording—and 1929—when she left the blues scene—she made close to thirty hit records and traveled the New York–San Francisco vaudeville circuit in a private Pullman car with a banner proclaiming "Sippie Wallace—Texas Nightingale" draped along its side.

She emerged from retirement in 1965—at the urging of her manager—to the delight of audiences at blues festivals throughout the United States and Europe. In 1970 a stroke silenced her for two years, but in 1972 Sippie Wallace came back once again. The Texas Nightingale is still singing the blues.

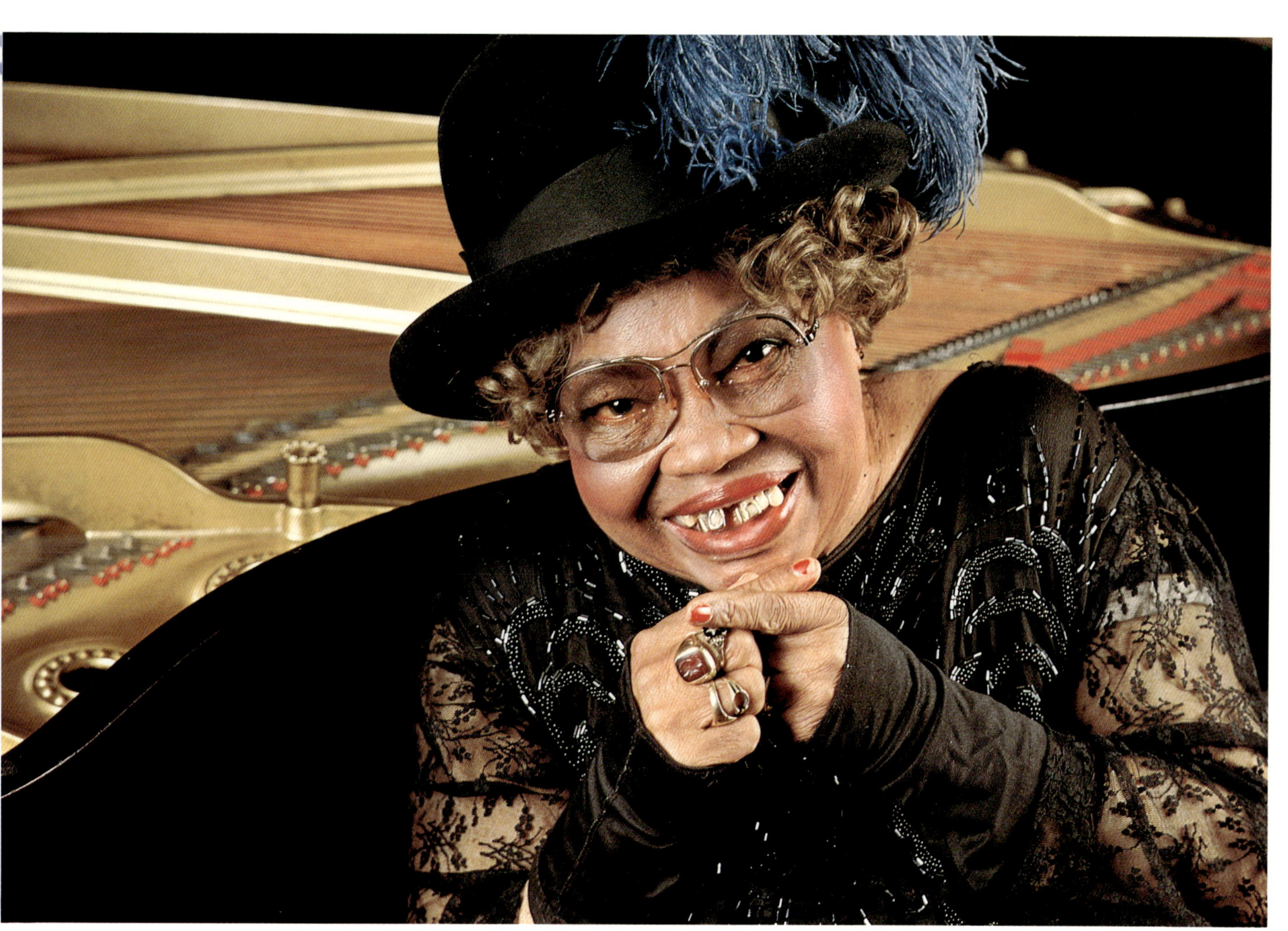

Mervyn LeRoy

October 15, 1900

From the slippers Dorothy wore in *The Wizard of Oz* to the Academy Award for *The House I Live In,* from a carving of the tugboat in *Tugboat Annie* to the black-and-white photographs of stars that cover the walls—Mervyn LeRoy's Los Angeles office is filled with Hollywood memories.

Mervyn LeRoy is one of the most prolific directors and producers Hollywood has ever known. He is most highly regarded for the racy, compelling films he directed during the Great Depression, including *Little Caesar, Five Star Final, Hard to Handle,* and *They Won't Forget.* Among his many other memorable films—encompassing almost every genre—are *Little Women, Quo Vadis, The Bad Seed,* and *Gypsy.* Fascinated by the theme, he is enthusiastically planning an epic Western that will be the ultimate cowboy and Indian saga.

Director-producer LeRoy offered me a bit of advice should I ever move to the other side of the camera. "Always," he said, giving me a demonstration, "wet your lips in front of the camera lens."

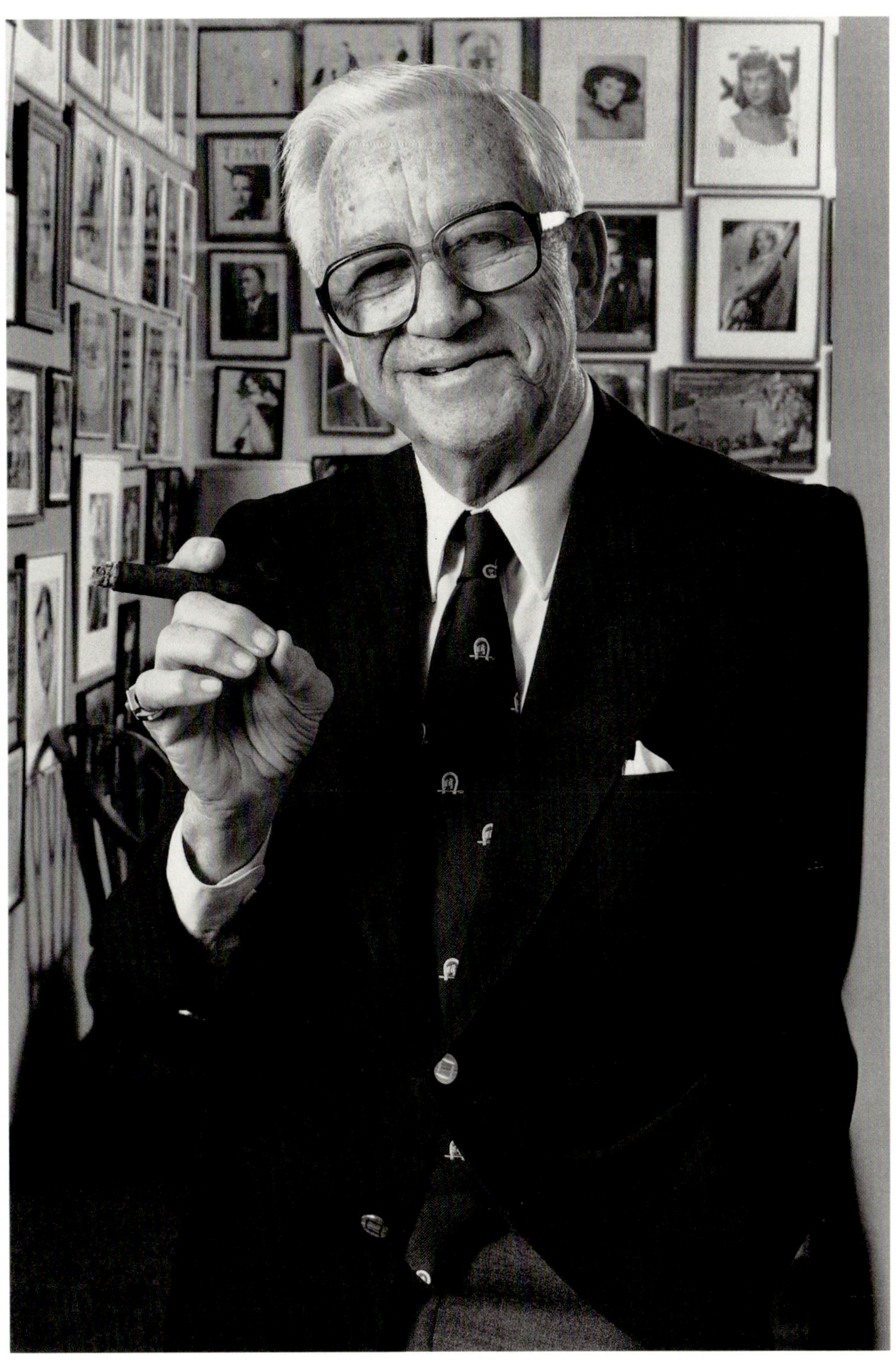

Roger Sessions

December 29, 1896

He wrote his first opera at ten; he entered Harvard University at fourteen. An eminent and prolific composer, university professor, and author of books on music theory and practice, Sessions has exerted a profound influence on several generations of American composers.

An organized man—who composes without an instrument—and winner of many awards, including a Pulitzer Prize, Sessions refuses to take the time to answer a letter.

Sessions told me he remembers a walk on January 1, 1900, when the family nurse accompanying the three-year-old Roger and his brother informed them that it was the first day of a new century. "Now if I just live to be a hundred and three," he mused, "I will have seen three centuries."

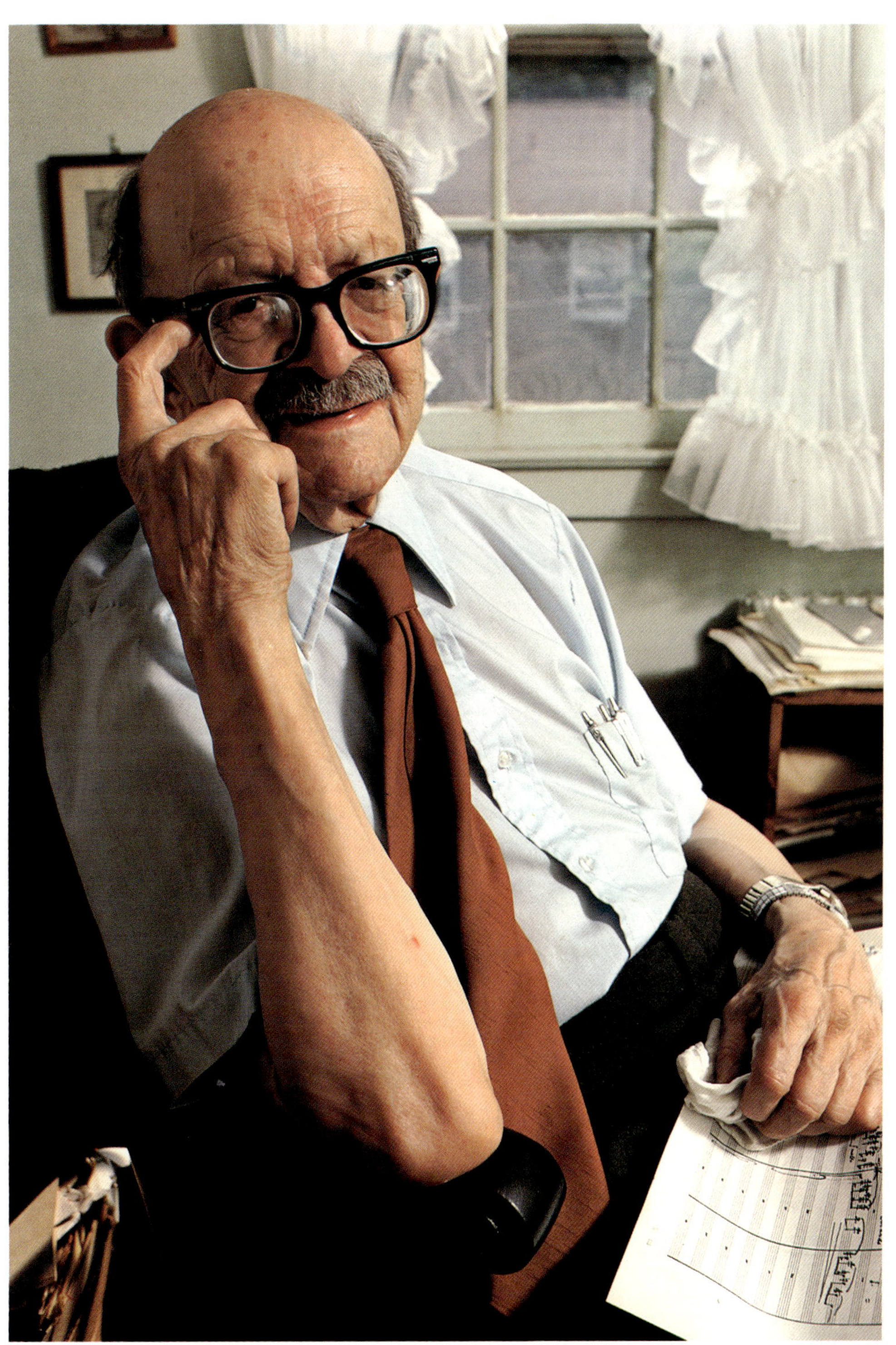

Kay Boyle

February 19, 1902

The role of the serious writer, Kay Boyle once wrote, is to be "the spokesman for those who remain inarticulate around him." Her stories bring to life the individual dramas of ordinary people caught up in the political and social upheavals that have shaken our world, from the rise of Nazism in Germany to the civil rights movement in the United States. Twice recipient of the O. Henry Award for short stories, she is also the author of novels, poetry, essays, and children's books.

Part of the Lost Generation of American writers in Paris in the 1920s, Kay Boyle lived and worked for several decades in Europe. She returned permanently to the United States in 1953.

One of the first authors to be published by the distinguished house of Alfred A. Knopf, she recalled a feature of the famous dinners served at the Knopf home: "I could always tell how well my book was doing," she reminisced, "by the wine that was served."

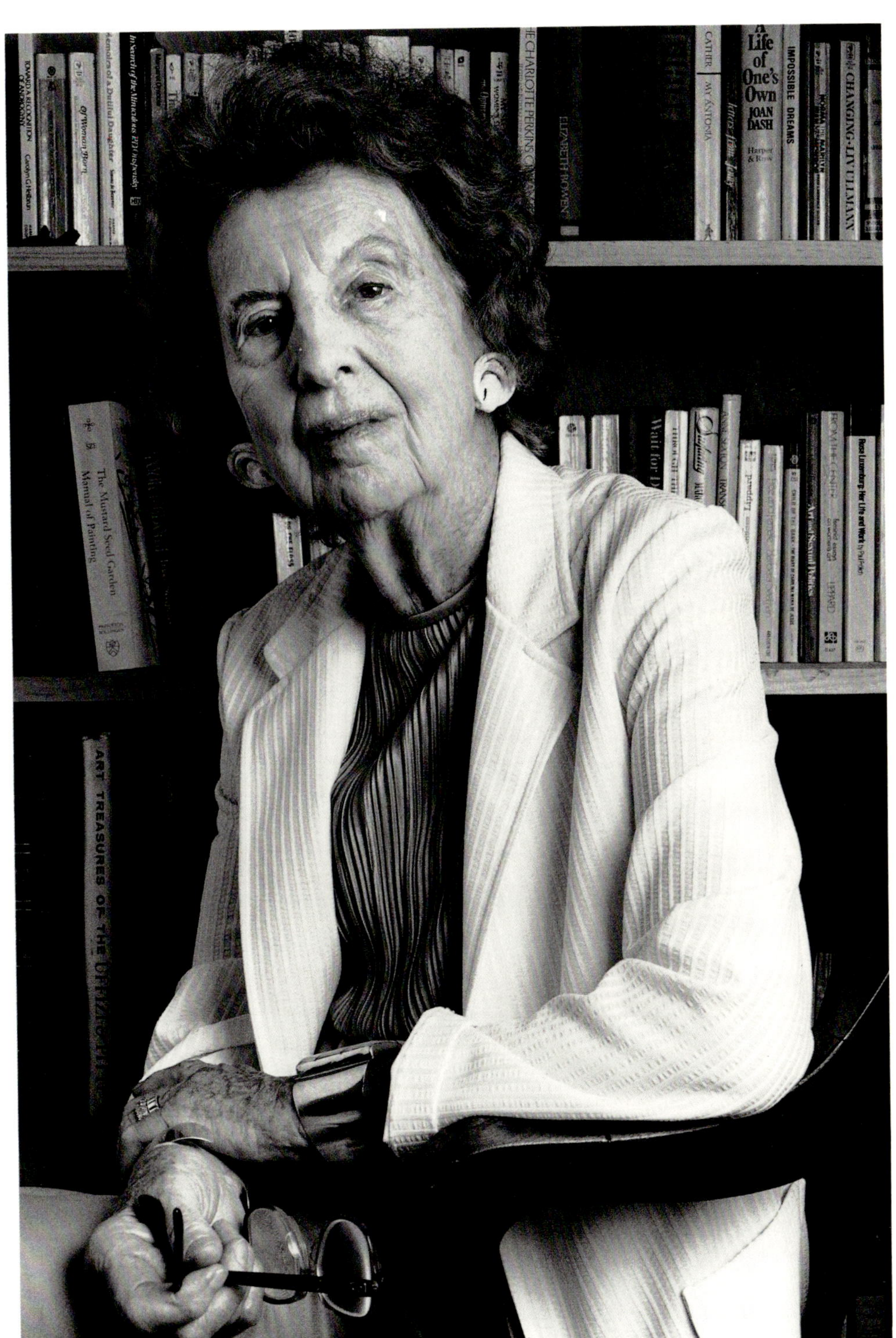
Memoirs of a Dutiful Daughter
CHARLOTTE PERKINS
ELIZABETH BOWEN
CATHER
MY ANTONIA
A Life of One's Own
JOAN DASH
Harper & Row
IMPOSSIBLE DREAMS
CHANGING · LIV ULLMANN
The Mustard Seed Garden Manual of Painting
Rosa Luxemburg Her Life and Work
ART TREASURES OF THE

Ray Arcel

August 30, 1899

When Ray Arcel guided Roberto Duran to his spectacular victory over Sugar Ray Leonard and the world welterweight championship in 1980, it was one more success. Fifty-six years earlier he had guided Abe Goldstein to his world bantamweight title. Between Goldstein and Duran, Ray trained a string of seventeen other world champions. After Duran, Ray said, "I've stopped counting."

Ray Arcel grew up in New York's Harlem when the city was the undisputed fight capital of the world. He started boxing in the local fight clubs as a teenager but quickly became fascinated by the trainers who could turn a street fighter into a professional boxer.

His reputation is based on his credo that the most important interest of the trainer is "the good and welfare of the boxer." I had to coax Ray to smile for his photo because he maintains that boxing is serious business.

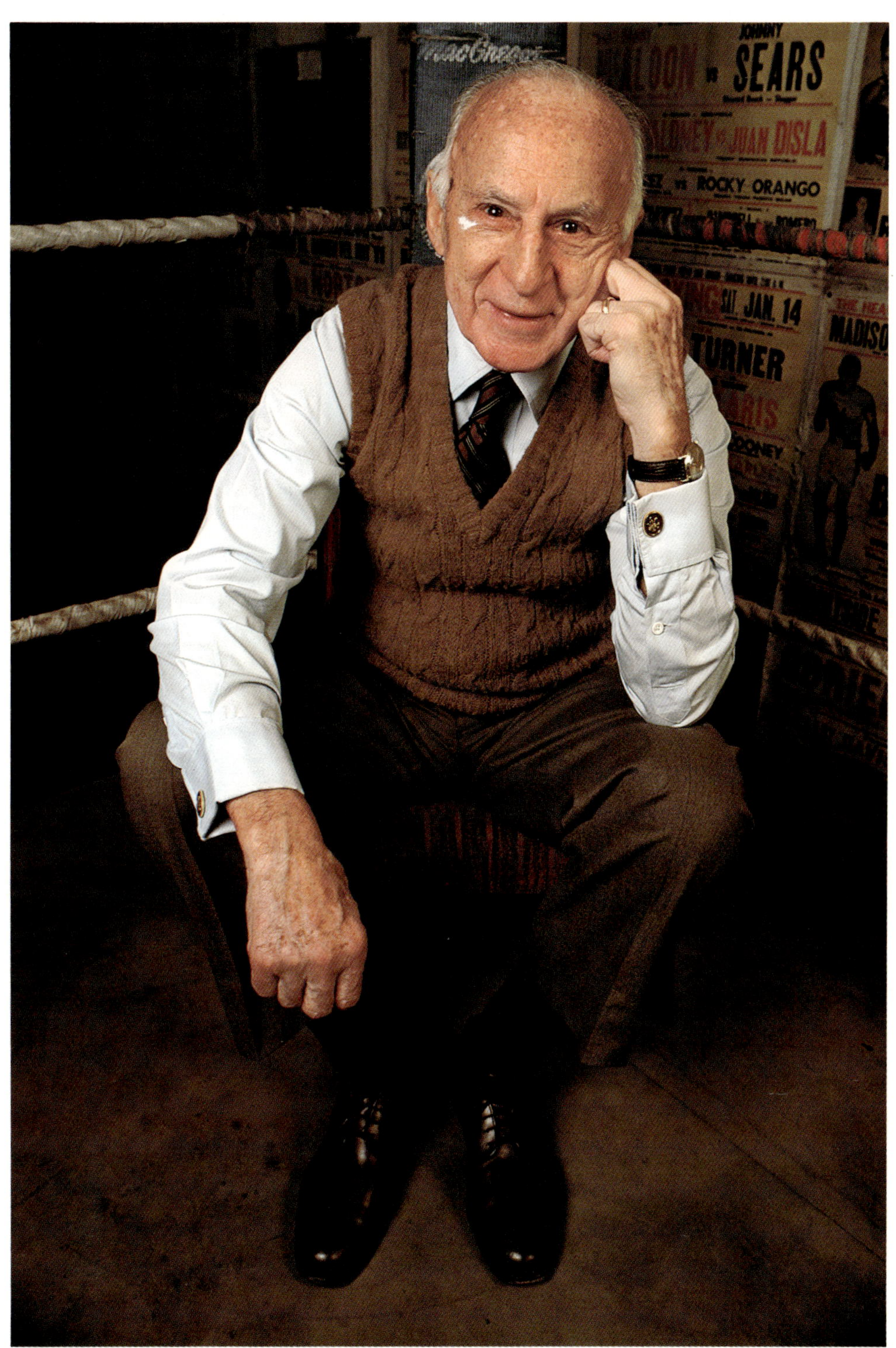
JOHNNY
SEARS
JUAN DISLA
ROCKY ORANGO
SAT. JAN. 14
TURNER

Ansel Adams

February 20, 1902

Ansel Adams's black-and-white prints are of extraordinary clarity and depict the dignity, strength, and beauty of nature untouched by man. He first took up a camera as a teenager to record the splendor of the mountains he loved to climb, and for more than six decades he has been an active conservationist fighting to preserve that wilderness.

Ansel is one of a handful of twentieth-century photographers credited with elevating photography from hobby to art. His prints command top prices.

Shooting a photographer as famous as Ansel Adams was intimidating. He understood my nervousness and he did his best to put me at ease—swapping stories and treating me as equal and friend. But as the session progressed, Ansel—one of photography's finest technicians—could not resist offering specific suggestions and guessing my f-stop and shutter speed.

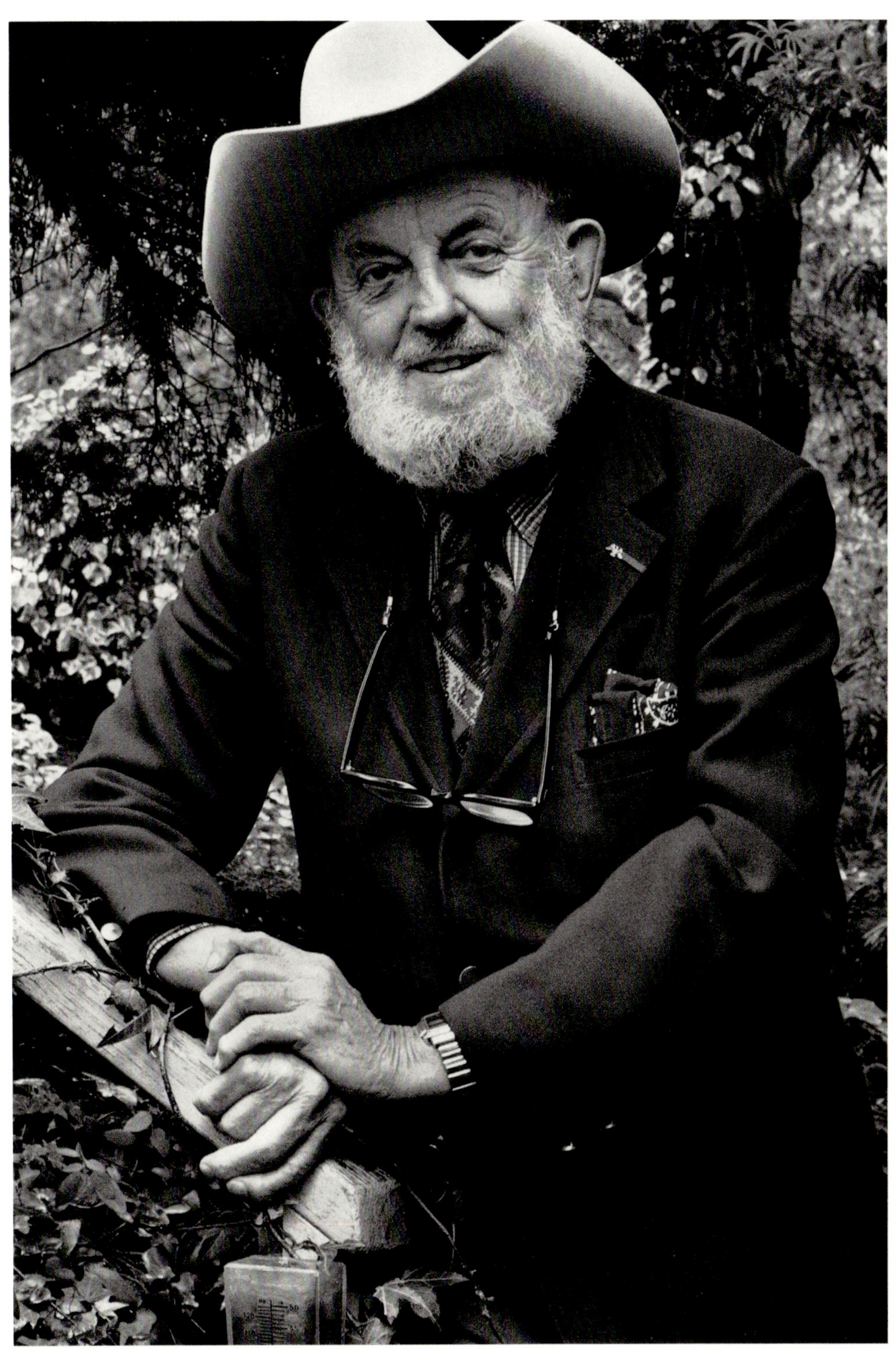

Sammy Fain

June 17, 1902

Every day, somewhere in the United States, someone is singing one of the countless songs of Sammy Fain—*I'll Be Seeing You, April Love, Tender Is the Night, Wedding Bells Are Breaking Up That Old Gang of Mine, Let a Smile Be Your Umbrella,* his two Oscar winners, *Love Is a Many Splendored Thing* and *Secret Love.*

Born in New York City, Sammy taught himself to play the piano and to write music. He began composing songs in high school, but it wasn't until 1925, while working in a vaudeville act, that Sammy published his first hit song, *Nobody Knows What a Red-Headed Mama Can Do.*

A peppy octogenarian, Sammy Fain works away. He has developed a real fondness for royalties. "That's what keeps me alive," he says with a grin.

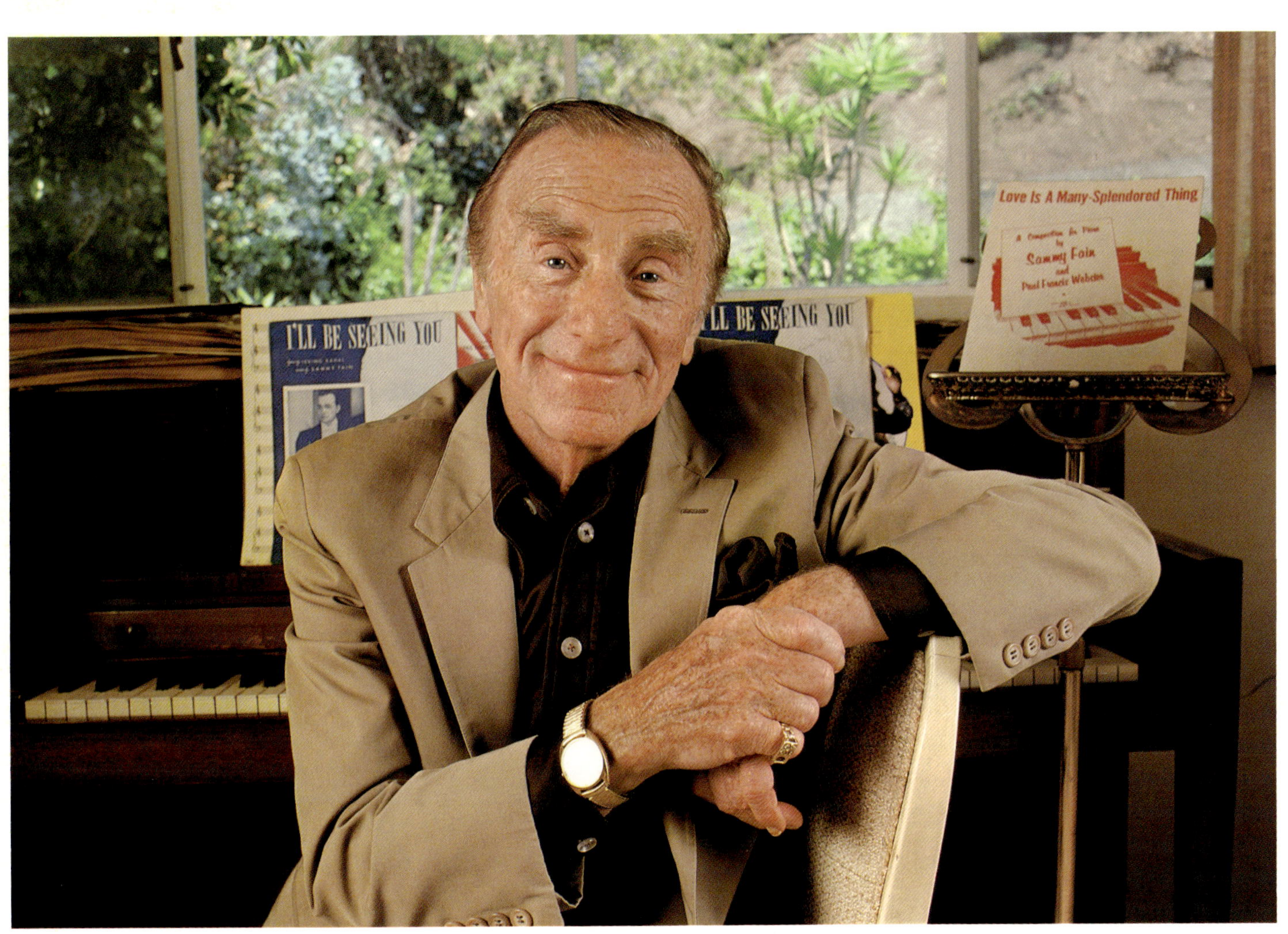
I'LL BE SEEING YOU
Love Is A Many-Splendored Thing
Sammy Fain
and
Paul Francis Webster

Harry Bridges

July 28, 1901

Harry Bridges is a tough, aggressive union man, but that is not the side he showed. I saw a gentle and smiling man, relaxed in his home, reminiscing about his life and at work on his autobiography.

The story of this feisty former Australian seaman is the story of the dockworkers on the West Coast of the United States. Harry Bridges went to sea at the age of sixteen. In 1920 he left his ship in San Francisco—in the city and country that became his new home. By the early 1930s he was leading a rank-and-file revolt against the corrupt leadership of the dockworkers' union—a revolt that culminated in the historic 1934 San Francisco General Strike.

The revolt also led to the formation of the International Longshoremen's and Warehousemen's Union (ILWU), which Bridges led as president for forty-three years, earning himself a reputation as one of the most militant, progressive, and honest labor leaders in the United States.

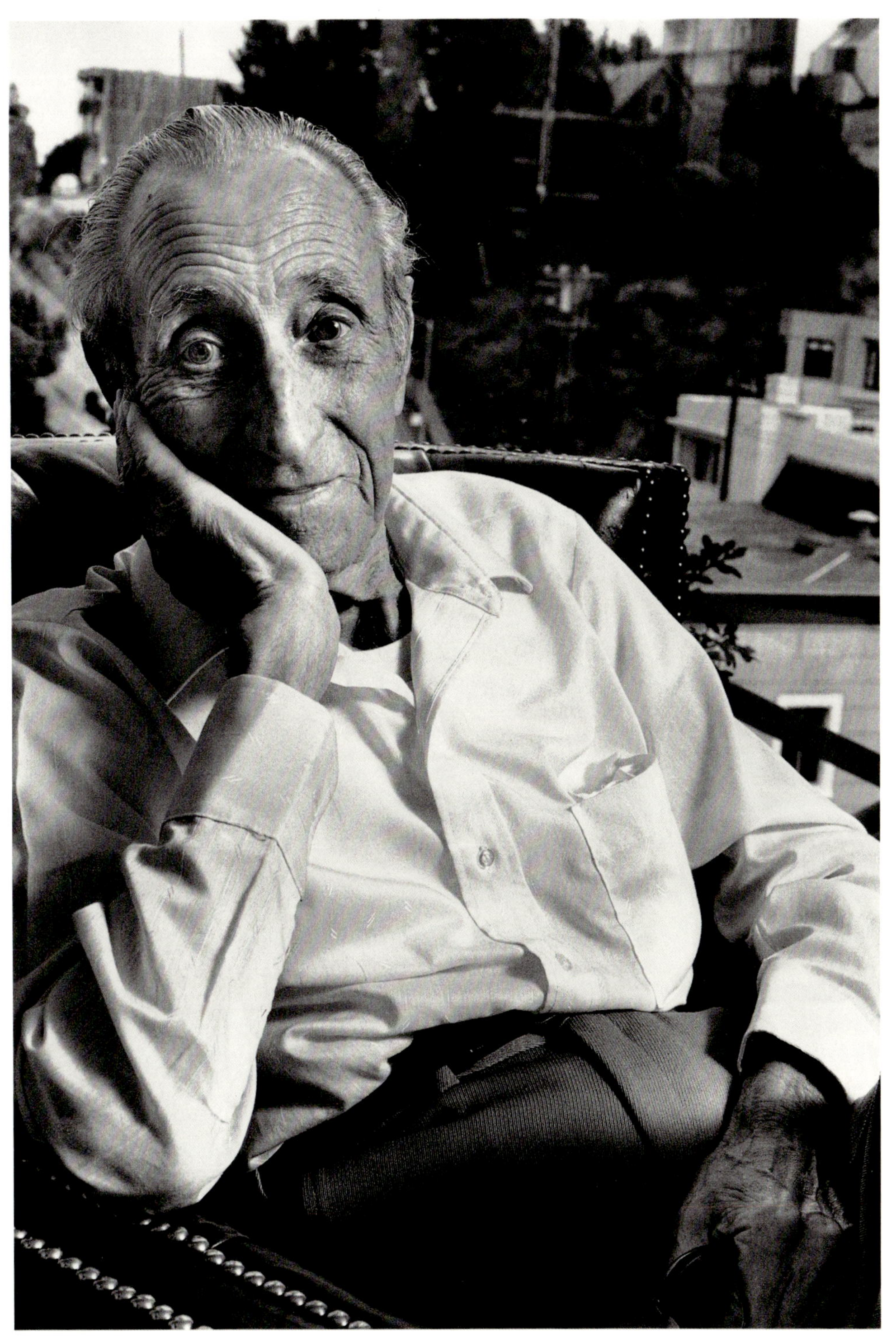

Jacques-Henri Lartigue

June 13, 1894

The wondrous, childlike quality of his photographs is also the outstanding trait of the man himself. Jacques-Henri Lartigue, whose photographs of French high society in the early decades of the twentieth century have been exhibited and widely reproduced in the United States, has been called the world's greatest amateur photographer.

The son of a wealthy French family, Lartigue was given a camera at the age of seven. He immediately began taking photographs whose freshness and originality are a continual delight. While it is photography that has won him renown, Lartigue insists that his profession is painting and that photography is a hobby. Being an amateur, he says, has allowed him to photograph only what he chooses!

The spry and lively Lartigue gives his age as "nine years—plus eighty." It is an accurate description of the joy and enthusiasm with which this octogenarian looks at the world.

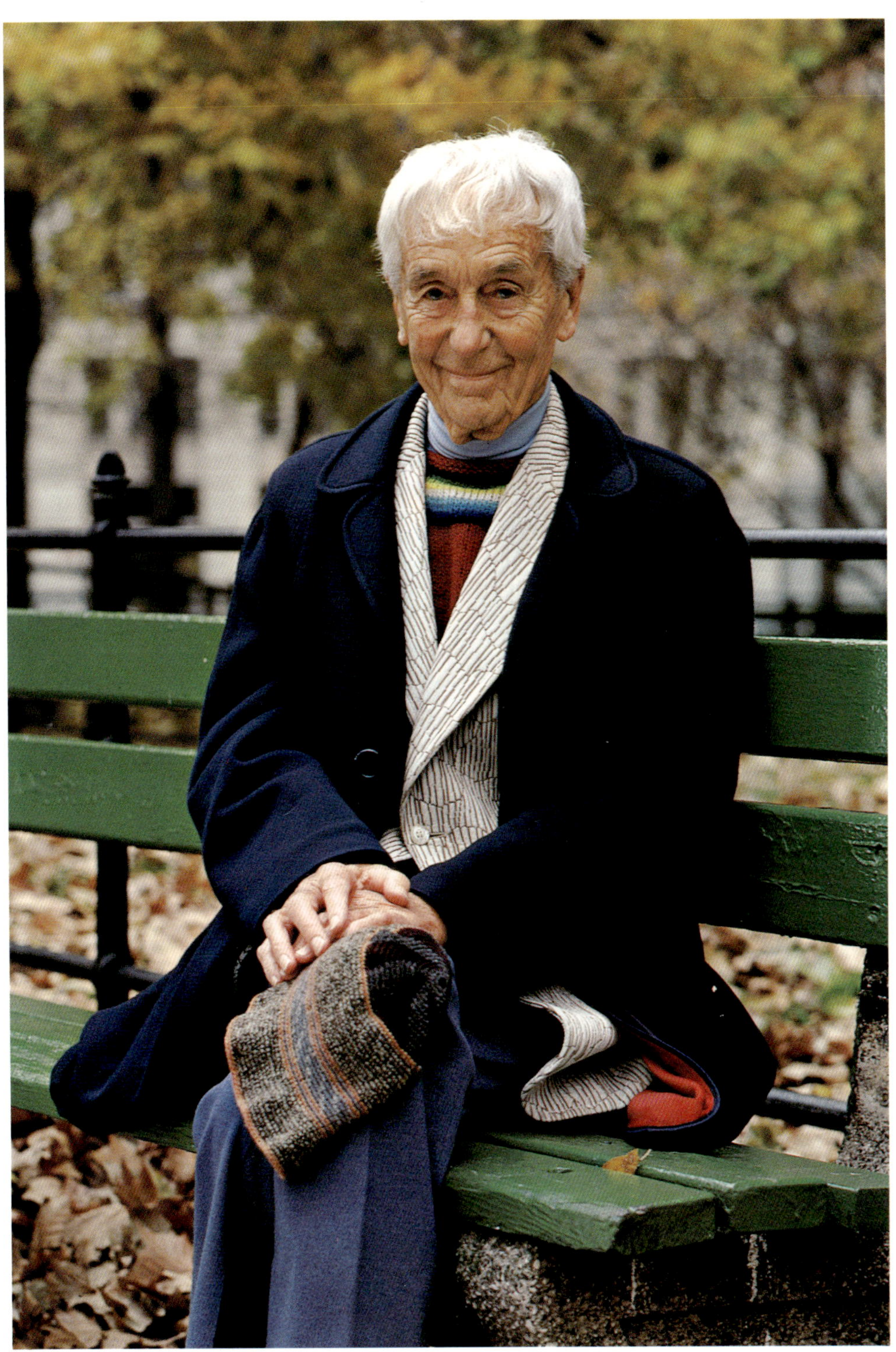

Corliss Lamont

March 28, 1902

Nothing," Corliss Lamont said, "gives me greater pleasure than a good fight for a good cause." And to this distinguished civil libertarian, philosopher, and author, it never mattered if the cause was unpopular.

Lamont's refusal to cooperate with the McCarthy committee in the 1950s; his successful fight in the 1960s against the post-master general's registration of citizens receiving mail from communist countries; and his winning battle in the 1970s to halt the Central Intelligence Agency's opening of mail are three instances of his never-ending defense of American freedoms. Despite substantial inherited wealth, he has always worked, teaching philosophy at several prestigious universities.

Corliss Lamont is also a man with a zest for life. An avid skier and tennis player through his seventy-eighth year, he is a lover of good food, dancing, and singing—in fact he once recorded an album of his favorite songs.

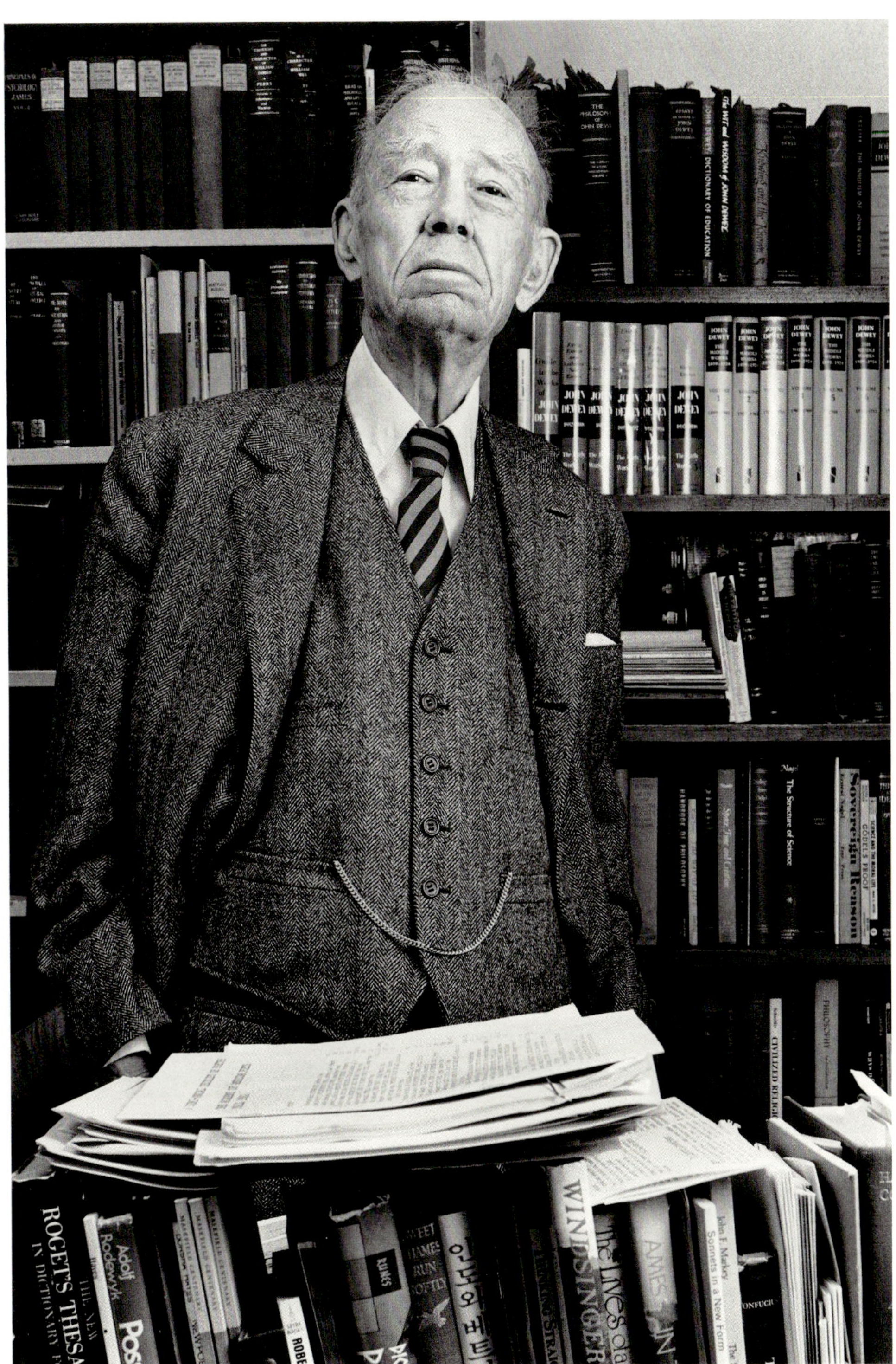

The WIT and WISDOM of JOHN DEWEY
DICTIONARY OF EDUCATION
JOHN DEWEY
The Structure of Science
Sovereign Reason
HANDBOOK OF PHILOSOPHY
THE NEW
Adolf Rodewyk
SWEET THAMES RUN SOFTLY
John F. Markey
Sonnets in a New Form

Alice Neel

January 28, 1900

Who else at the age of eighty would paint a nude self-portrait? Only Alice Neel, an outspoken, spirited, and "liberated" woman—long before that term was in vogue. Her life, lived without regard for the current fashion in either politics or art, has often been hard. But she voices no regrets for the independence she has so fiercely maintained.

Alice is fascinated by people. And while she has painted cityscapes, landscapes, and still lifes, it is for her unconventional, penetrating portraits that she is renowned. The faces—of celebrities and ordinary people alike—mirror what Alice sees in their souls and depict the price each subject has paid to an often harsh society.

Her apartment on New York's Upper West Side is crammed with her paintings; they line the narrow corridor, making it difficult to squeeze past. She is always at work and every visitor becomes a potential portrait. Painting each new face with words, she singles out and verbalizes the characteristics that will dominate her canvas. The vitality of her interpretations and the originality of her viewpoint are as strong as ever.

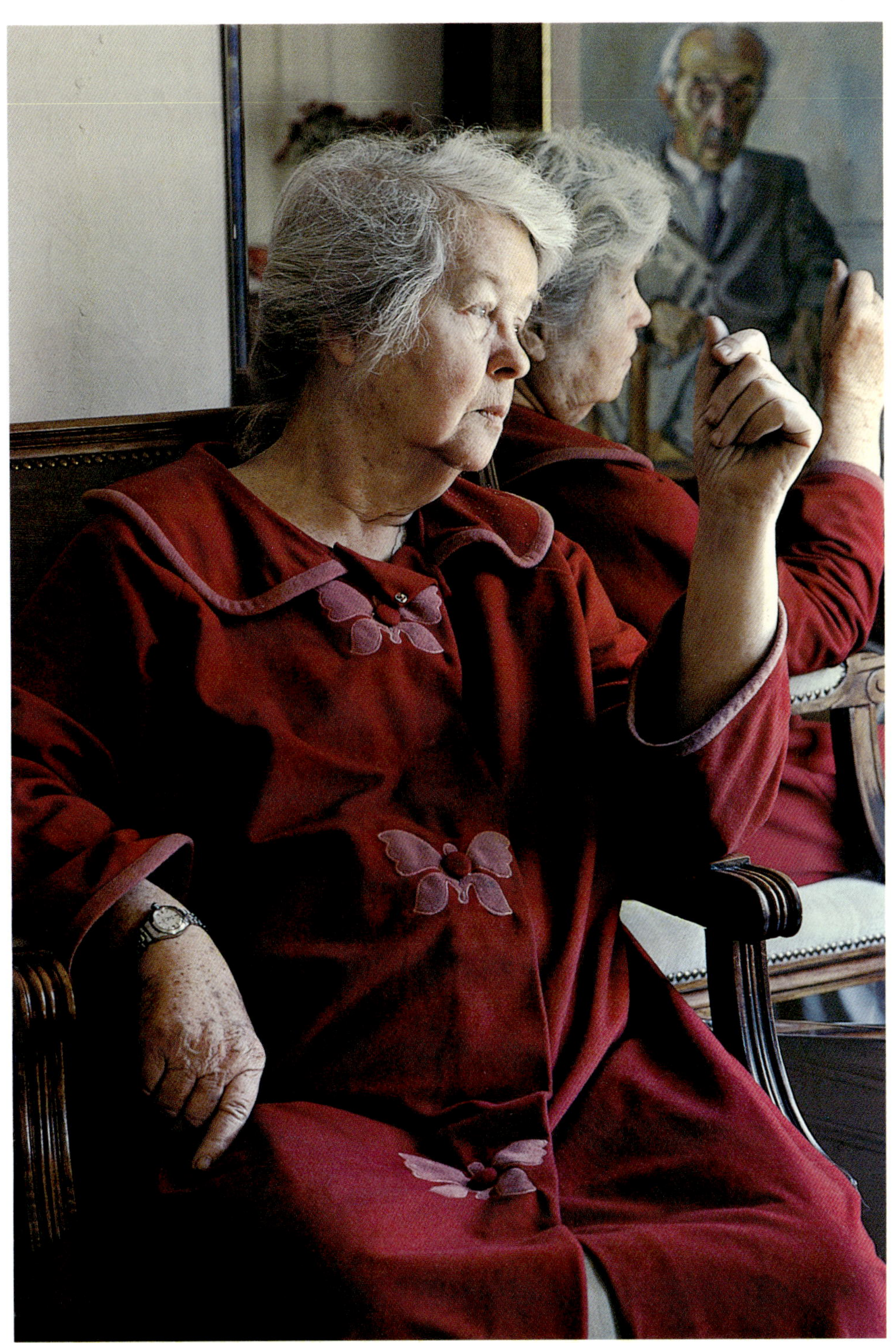

Art Rooney

January 27, 1901

At Three Rivers Stadium in Pittsburgh, he is known as the "Chief"—the man who stuck by his Steelers through many long and dreary seasons until they emerged in the mid-1970s as the top team in the National Football League (NFL).

Rooney started out as a baseball and football player. In 1933 he invested twenty-five hundred dollars in the Pittsburgh franchise of the NFL, and he has watched professional football go from the struggle to meet weekly payrolls to the multimillion-dollar business it is today. Not only is he the owner and president of the Pittsburgh Steelers, he is a boxing promoter, breeder of champion horses, and, with his sons, the owner of several racetracks.

"People don't understand my lingo. I talk sports slang," he said. But whatever the language, he reflects the warmth and loyalty for which he is known: "It's been a wonderful eighty-one years . . . all winners, no losers—all friends, no enemies."

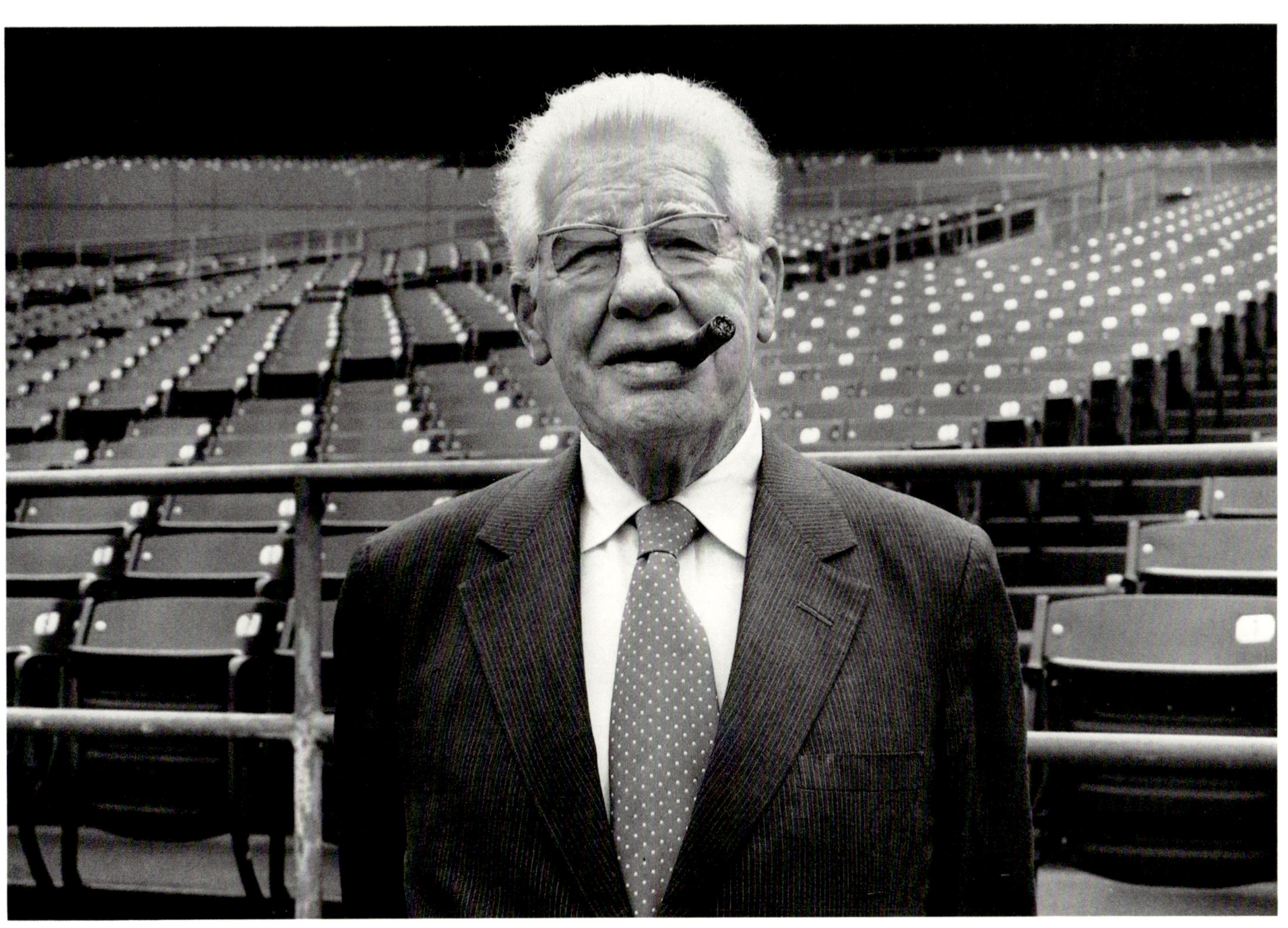

Sir Rudolf Bing

January 9, 1902

"All my life up to 1949 could be seen as the proper preparation for being manager of the Metropolitan," wrote Sir Rudolf Bing in his memoir, *Five Thousand Nights at the Opera.* As general manager of New York's Metropolitan Opera for twenty-two years, Sir Rudolf—often called "the autocrat of the Met"—was a controversial figure. But even his critics concede that his artistic influence and fresh approaches revitalized the Met.

Born in Vienna, Sir Rudolf worked with concert artists in Austria and then Germany. When Hitler came to power he moved to England, where he worked with several opera companies. In 1950 he came to New York for the start of his long career at the Metropolitan. Sir Rudolf is particularly proud of having hired Marian Anderson—the first black singer to appear with the company.

Since his retirement from the Met, Sir Rudolf has continued to work with opera singers. A composed and aristocratic man, he has a way of getting things done—he simply claps his hands loudly, and everybody gets moving.

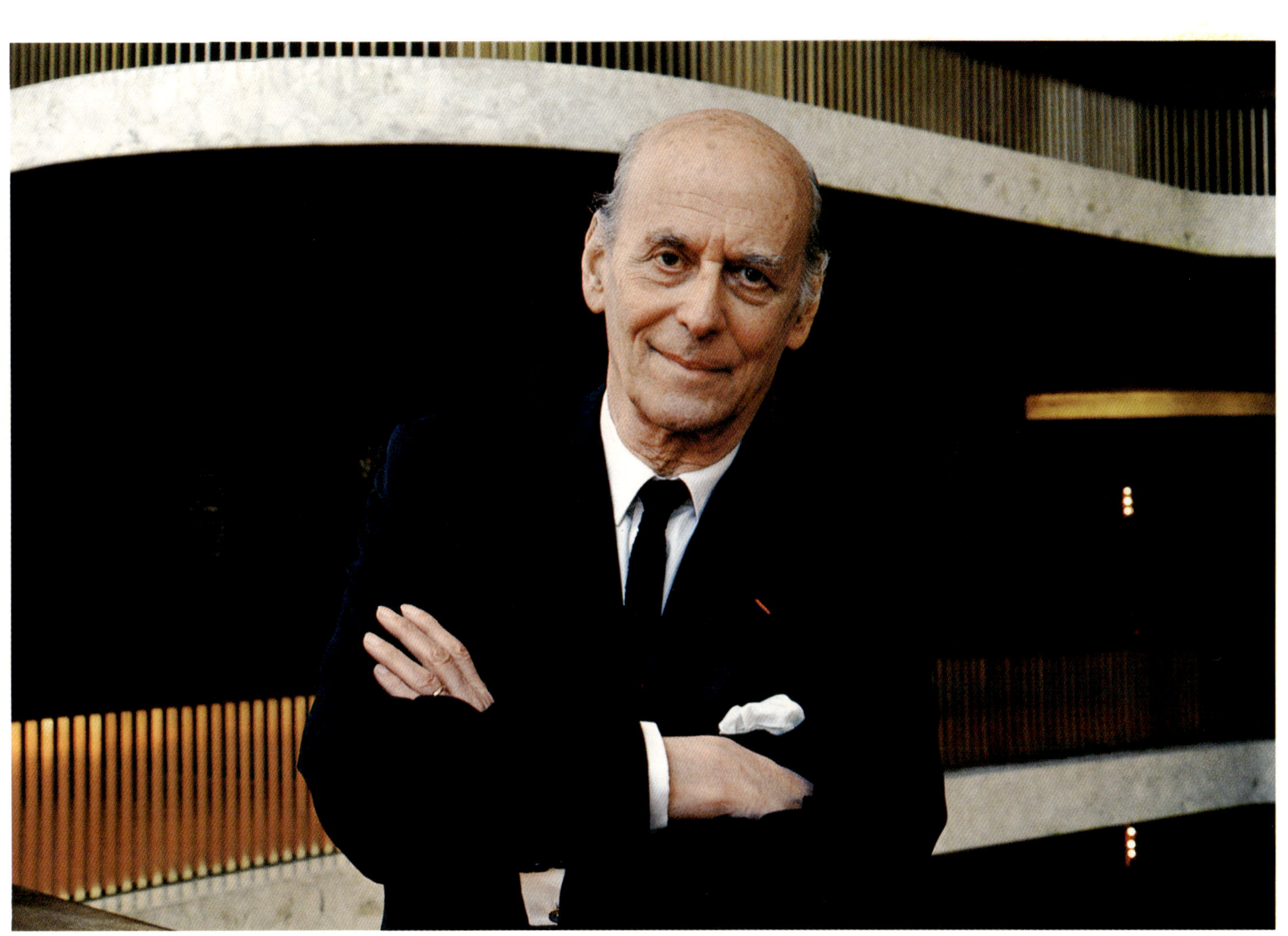

George T. Delacorte, Jr.

June 20, 1894

Watching the children play in the Alice in Wonderland Playground in New York City's Central Park, George Delacorte remarked, "Kids say the same thing in every language: 'Look, mommy, look at me!'" George Thomas Delacorte, Jr., the father of six, grandfather of seventeen, and great-grandfather of two, should know—he has spent much of the last thirty years providing oases of pleasure for New York children and their parents.

The Alice in Wonderland sculpture is only one of Delacorte's many gifts to his native city. The Delacorte Theater in Central Park, the automated glockenspiel above the Central Park Zoo, and a number of magnificent fountains throughout the city are all presents from "New York's own Santa Claus."

George Delacorte founded Dell Publishing in 1921; and under his astute leadership the company became one of the largest and most diversified mass-market publishers in the world. Today he offers words of encouragement for his juniors: "The first ninety years are the hardest."

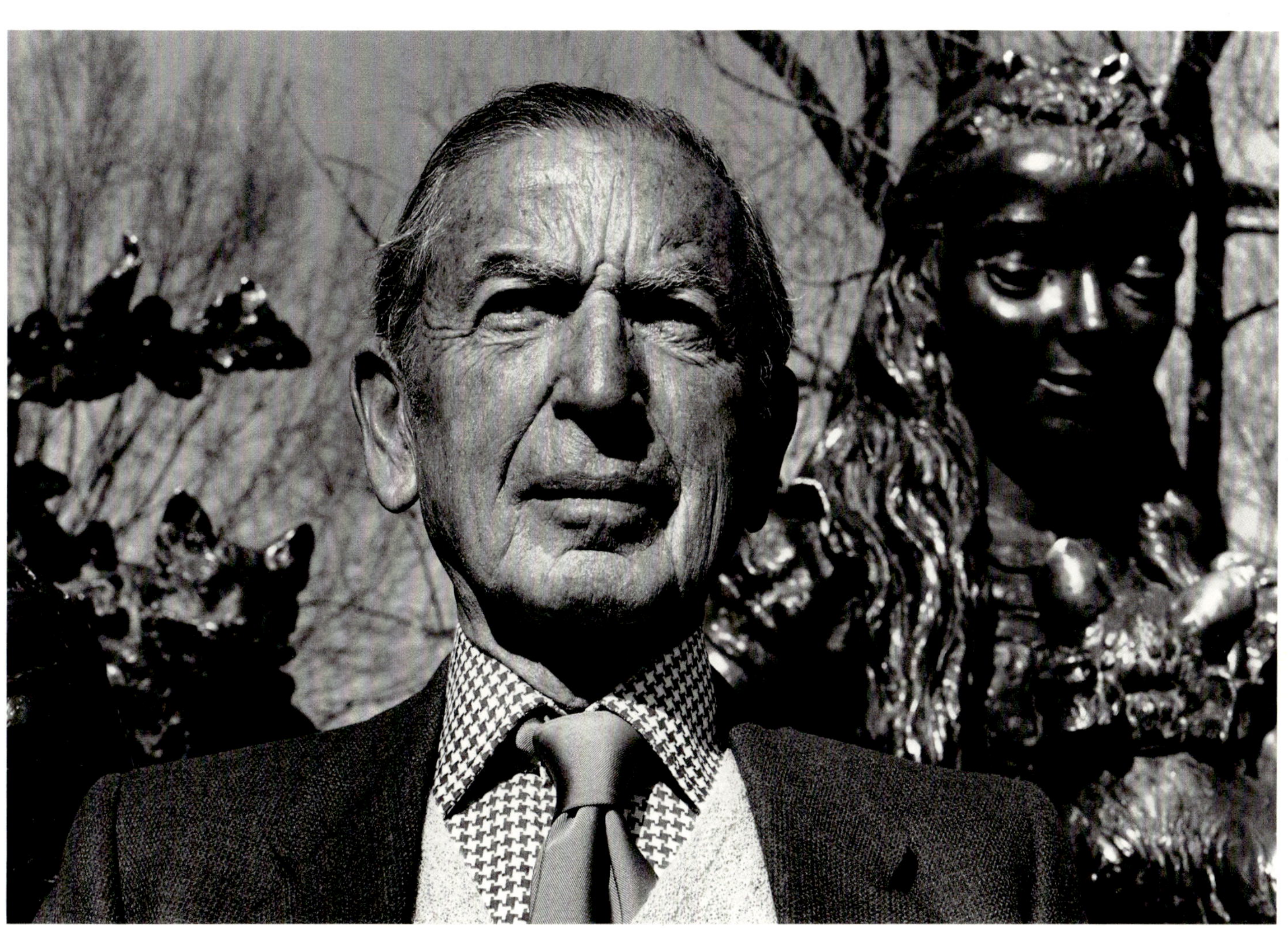

Rudy Vallee

July 28, 1901

The first singer to be called a "crooner" and the first to cause mass swooning among his audiences, Rudy Vallee is remembered by a generation of American women as "The Vagabond Lover"—the crooner with a megaphone.

Rudy achieved fame in New York City in 1928 through his radio broadcasts from the Heigh-Ho Club. A popular singer and bandleader on the screen, radio, and stage throughout the 1930s and 1940s, he proved himself an accomplished comedian as well. His return to Broadway in the 1961 hit musical *How to Succeed in Business Without Really Trying* won him plaudits from a new generation of theatergoers.

A visit to Rudy's home in the hills above Hollywood is a nostalgia-filled trip down memory lane. *My Time Is Your Time*—the title of his theme song—is emblazoned on the mat that greets you at his door. And the friendly and expansive host will escort you through the Rudy Vallee Hall of Fame beneath the tennis court. He will treat you to a one-man show and send you away with arms full of autographed souvenirs.

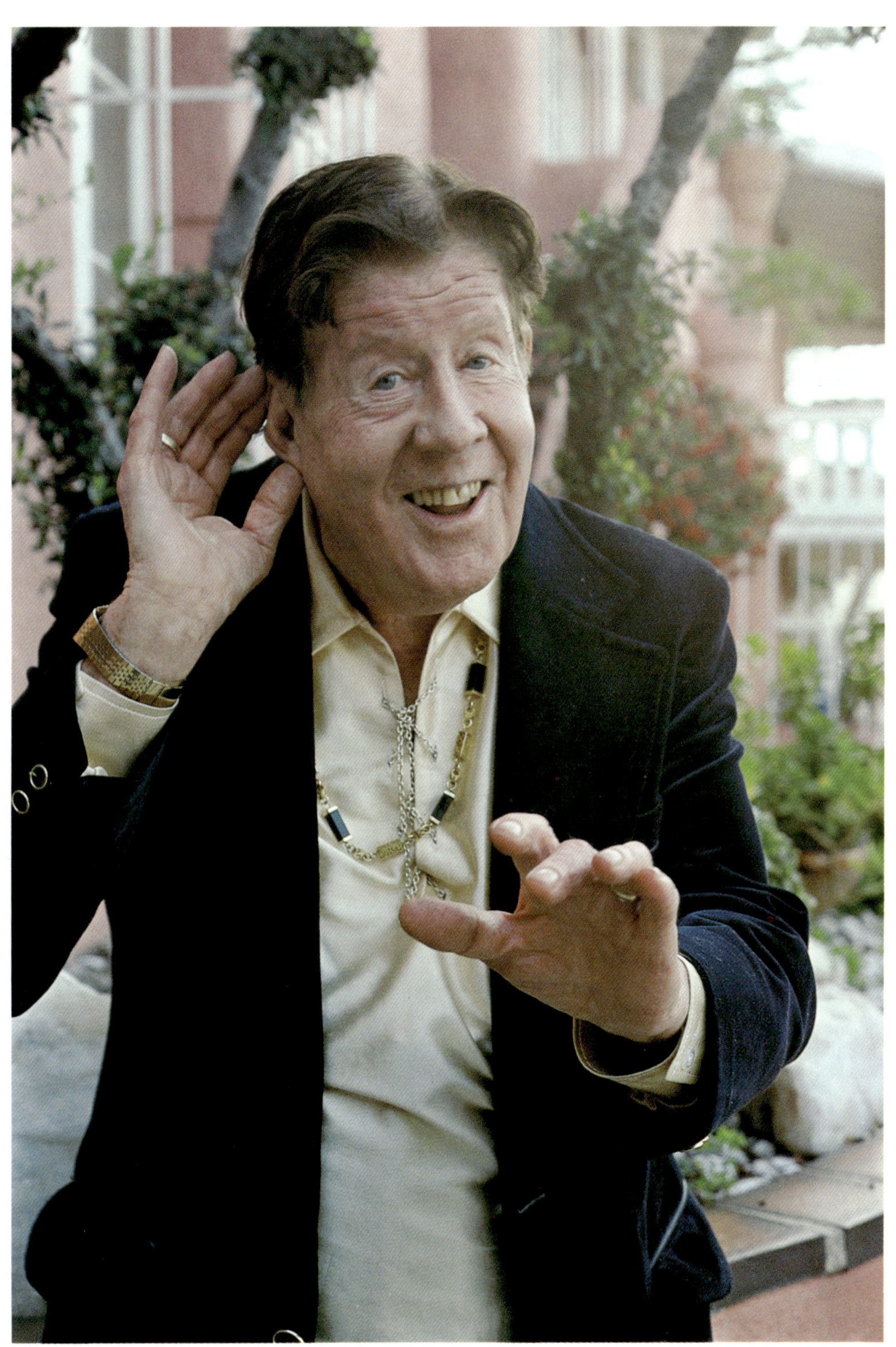

Anatole Vilzak

October 28, 1896

Although ballet dancers usually shun such gimmicky garb as rah-rah T-shirts, the "Viva Vilzak" shirt is a routine sight at the San Francisco School of Ballet. It testifies to the charm, style, and warmth of this veteran ballet star and sought-after teacher.

Vilzak first achieved fame in his native St. Petersburg, dancing with Tamara Karsavina. In 1921, after he and Ludmila Schollar, his wife and dancing partner, left Russia, they danced with the foremost ballet companies in Europe and the United States, including Sergei Diaghilev's Ballets Russes. As dancers and teachers, Vilzak and Schollar have made an unforgettable imprint on dancers and audiences on both sides of the Atlantic and as far as the shores of the Pacific.

Anatole Vilzak is always "on," whether teaching a class or sitting for a photograph. In his delightful accent, he shared with me a bit of his prescription for correcting his students with humor instead of rudeness. You don't call them "stupid," you call them "two-by-fours."

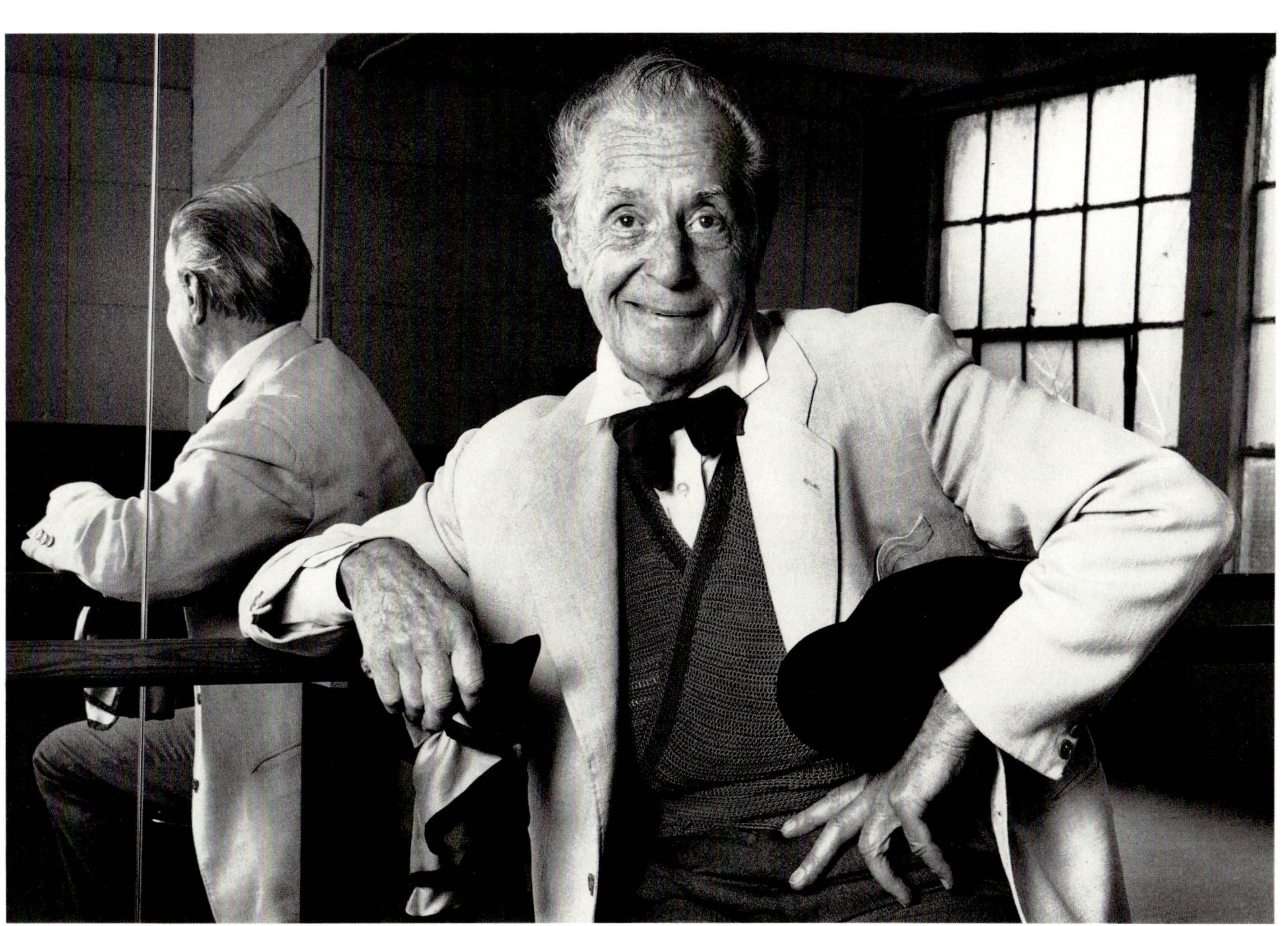

Cyril Magnin

July 6, 1899

Call Me Cyril, a Bay Area best-seller, is the autobiography of Cyril Magnin—San Francisco's most sought-after bachelor and a philanthropist on a substantial scale. He is also the city's chief of protocol, a role he created for himself twenty years ago following the death of his wife.

The debonair Cyril made a fortune by turning the retail clothing store he was given by his father into "the young Magnin's," the first store to go after the youth market aggressively. Since his appearance as the Pope in the film *Foul Play,* Cyril has added acting to his list of achievements.

His office, on the top floor of the Joseph Magnin headquarters, overlooks the Bay Bridge. During our photo session he shook his finger at me. I asked him what this meant. He chuckled. "You know," he said, "this comes from my law school days, when a professor told me always to address the jury with my index finger."

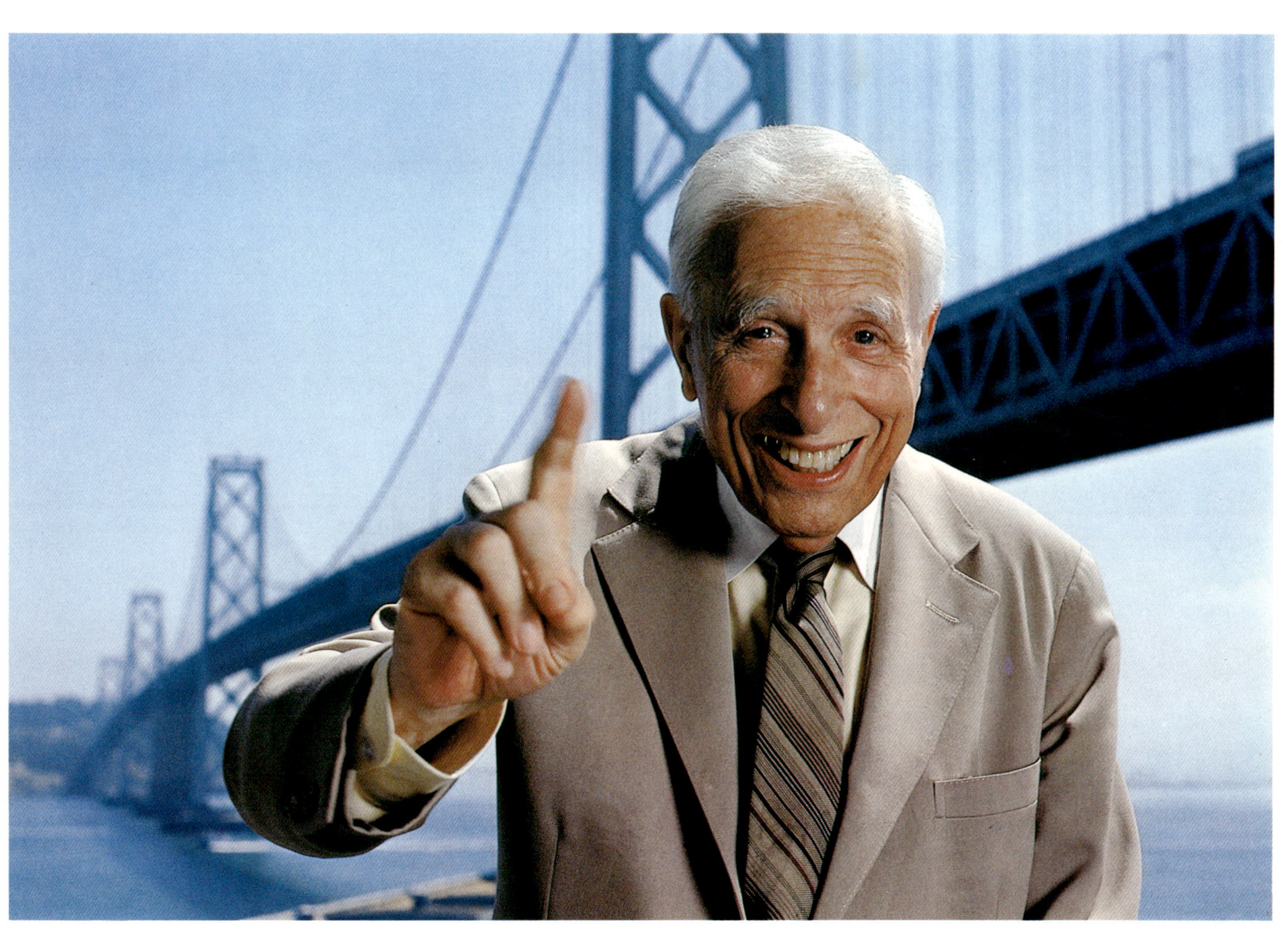

Harry L. Shapiro

March 19, 1902

Harry Shapiro began his career sixty years ago with a study of the mutinous crew of the *Bounty* and their Polynesian wives. His interest in racial and genetic characteristics and their mixtures has taken him around the world.

Chairman emeritus of the anthropology department at the American Museum of Natural History, professor emeritus at Columbia University, distinguished author and lecturer, Dr. Harry L. Shapiro is the dean of American physical anthropologists. He works in a sunny office at the top of the museum—and for two hours he kept me enthralled with his wonderful tales of exotic peoples and cultures in far corners of the globe.

To the New York Police Department, Dr. Shapiro is known as the man who can read bones. The police bring him fragments of skeletons from which he can tell the sex, race, and age of people of which the bones are the only remaining traces.

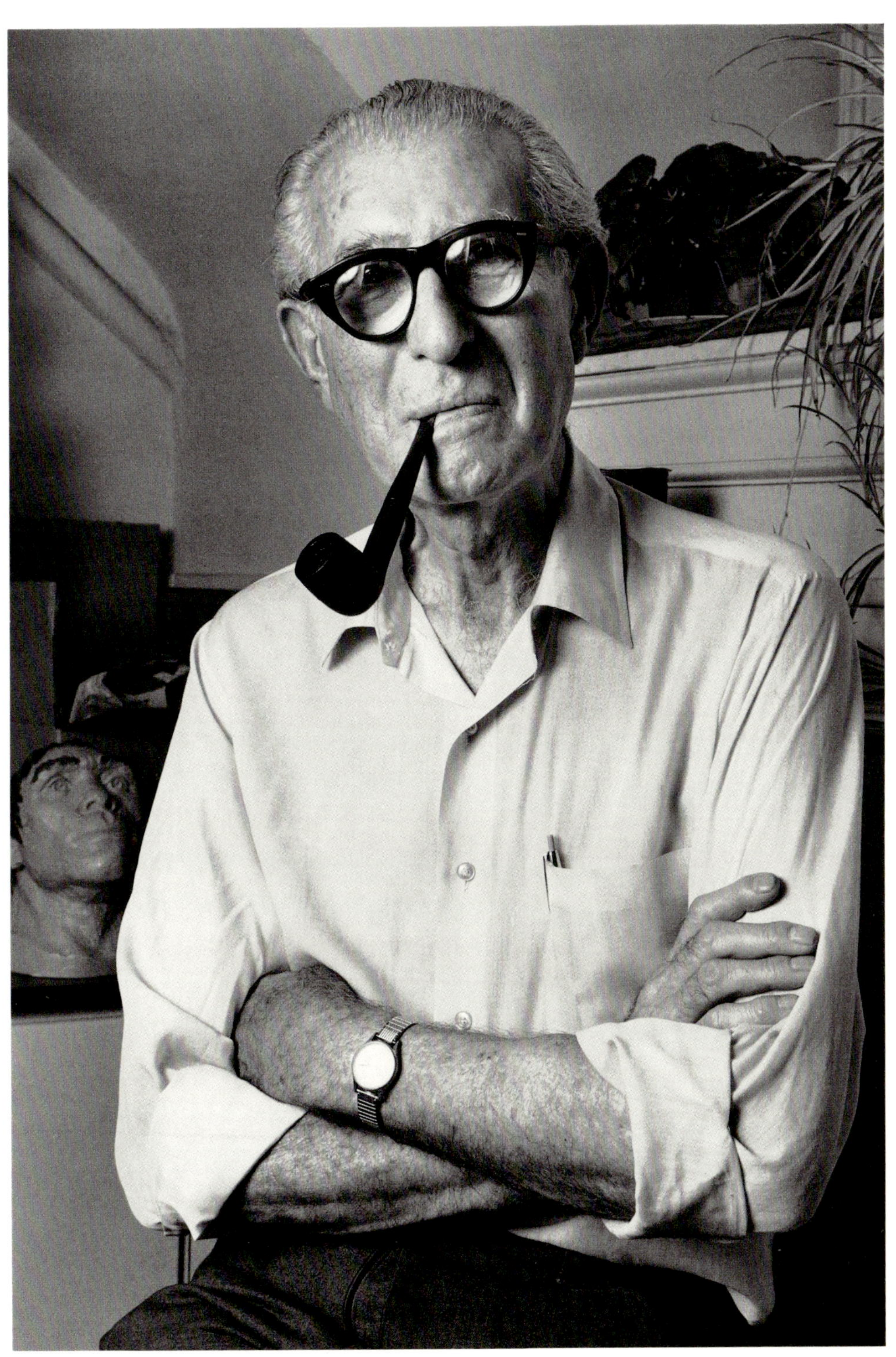

Max Lerner

December 20, 1902

The syndicated column Max Lerner writes three times a week for over a hundred journals nationwide is only one facet of an otherwise fully engaged professional life. In addition to his writing commitments, Lerner teaches psychology at the Graduate School of Human Behavior at the U.S. International University in San Diego and holds a chair in American Studies—a department he founded in the 1930s at Sarah Lawrence—at Notre Dame. In a long career marked by reflection and social commentary, Lerner has gone on to publish fifteen books, among them his 1957 classic *America as a Civilization.*

Being active is the only way of life for Max Lerner. "To live is to function," says Lerner. "If the unexamined life isn't worth living, the unlived life isn't worth examining."

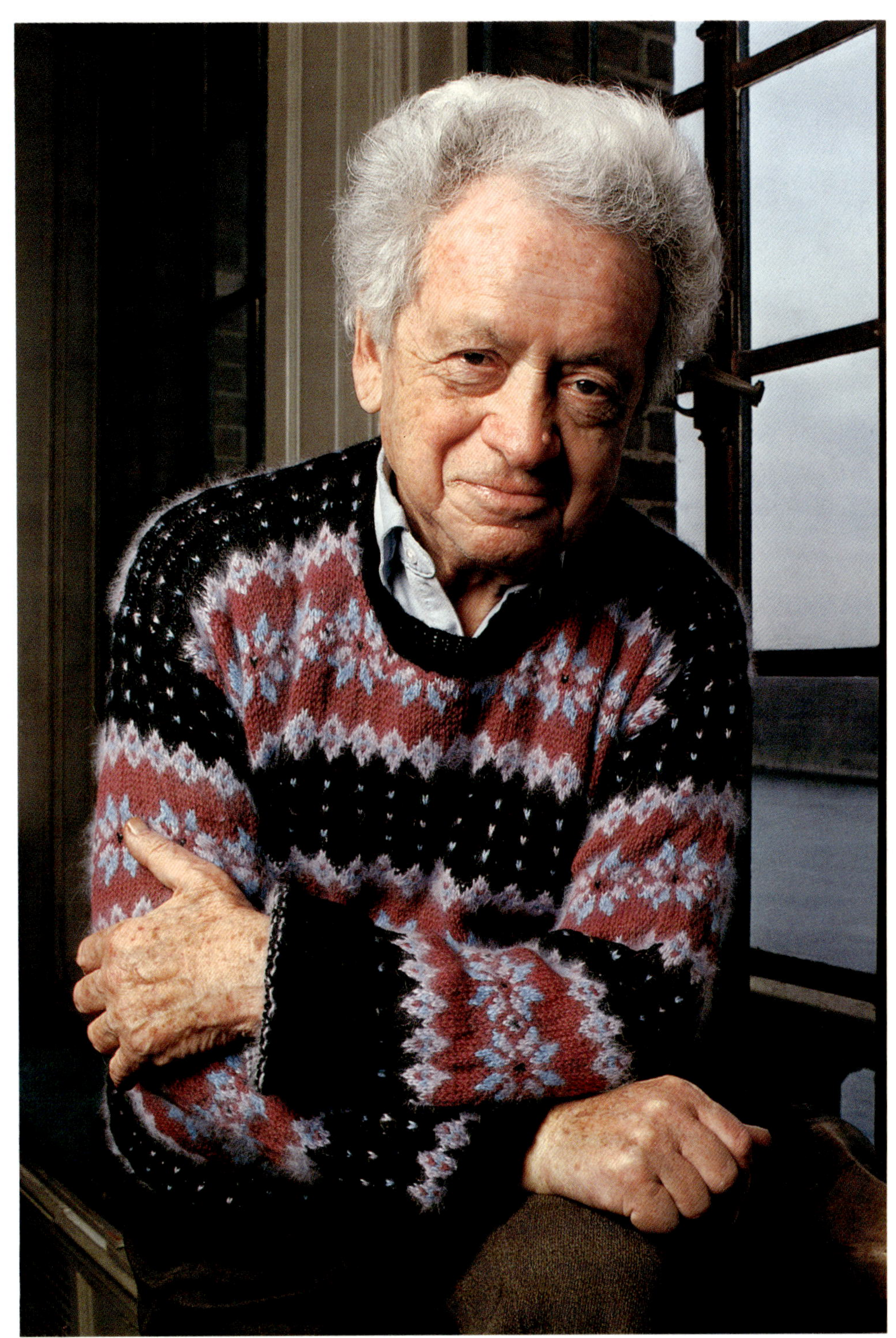

Morris Carnovsky

September 5, 1898

Morris Carnovsky is probably the most versatile and accomplished Shakespearean actor on the American stage. He considers the study, performance, and teaching of Shakespeare to be his life's work. His favorite Shakespearean roles are Shylock in *The Merchant of Venice,* Prospero in *The Tempest,* and the title role in *King Lear.*

Carnovsky has also acted in plays by other playwrights on Broadway and in films. A founding member of the Group Theater, he appeared in its productions of *Awake and Sing, Paradise Lost, Golden Boy, Rocket to the Moon,* and *Night Music,* among others.

The consummate actor, Carnovsky kept us both entertained throughout our photo session as he spoke lines—in Italian, French, and German—from roles he invented as he went along. Fully occupied with his teaching and acting, he jokingly showed me the book he means to write—still filled with blank pages waiting for him to slow down.

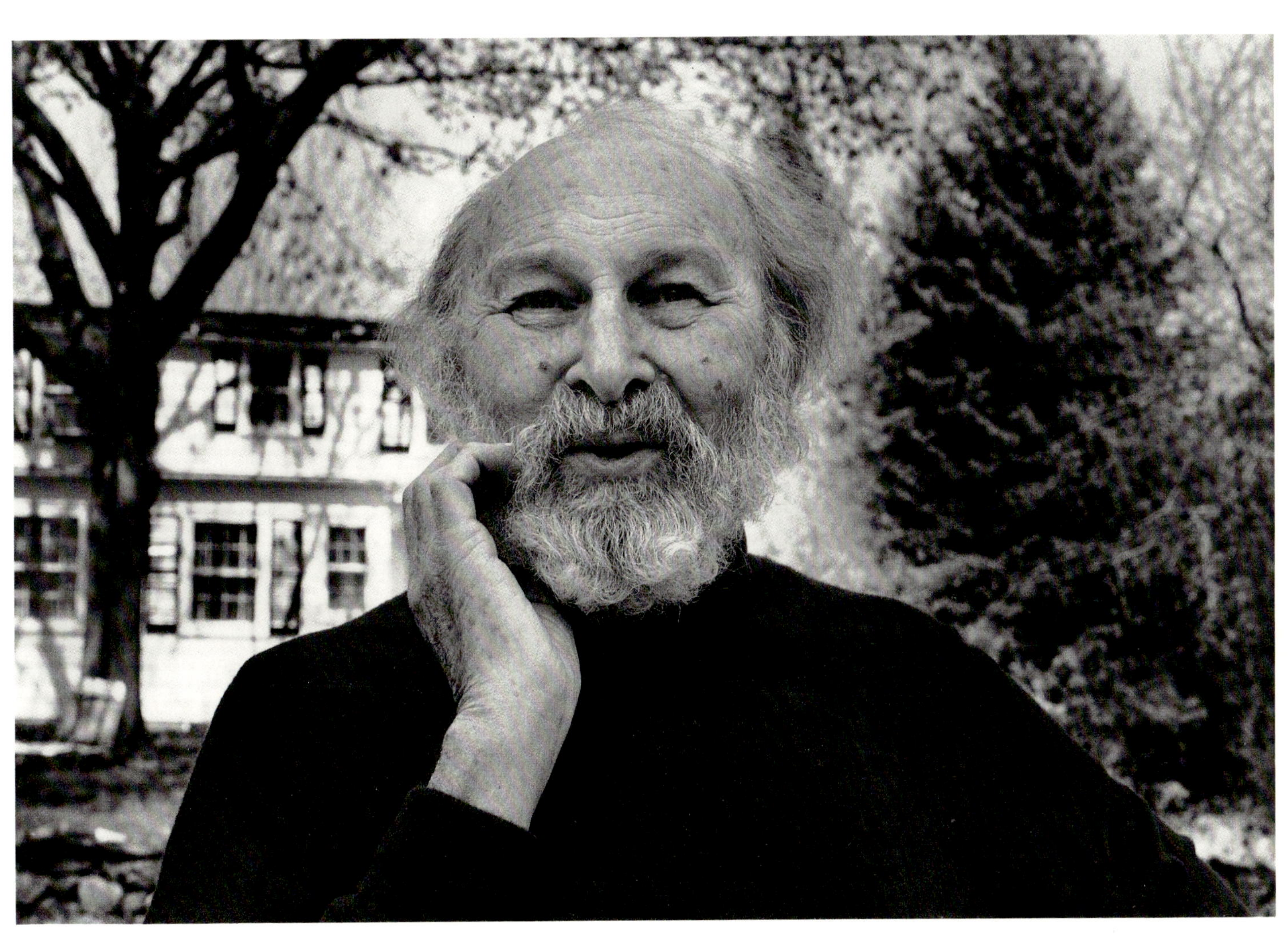

Kenneth Burke

May 5, 1897

He used to be known as "the critics' critic," because of his complex writing and formidable intellect. In addition to his work on the theory of literary criticism and on philosophy, he has written short stories, poetry, a novel, and music criticism.

Kenneth Burke is a man with sparkling eyes and a wonderful sense of humor, given to sprinkling his conversation with riddles. The neighborhood kids who hang around his rural home know him as "K. B."

According to K. B., "the cure for digging in the dirt is an idea. The cure for any idea is more ideas. The cure for all ideas is digging in the dirt."

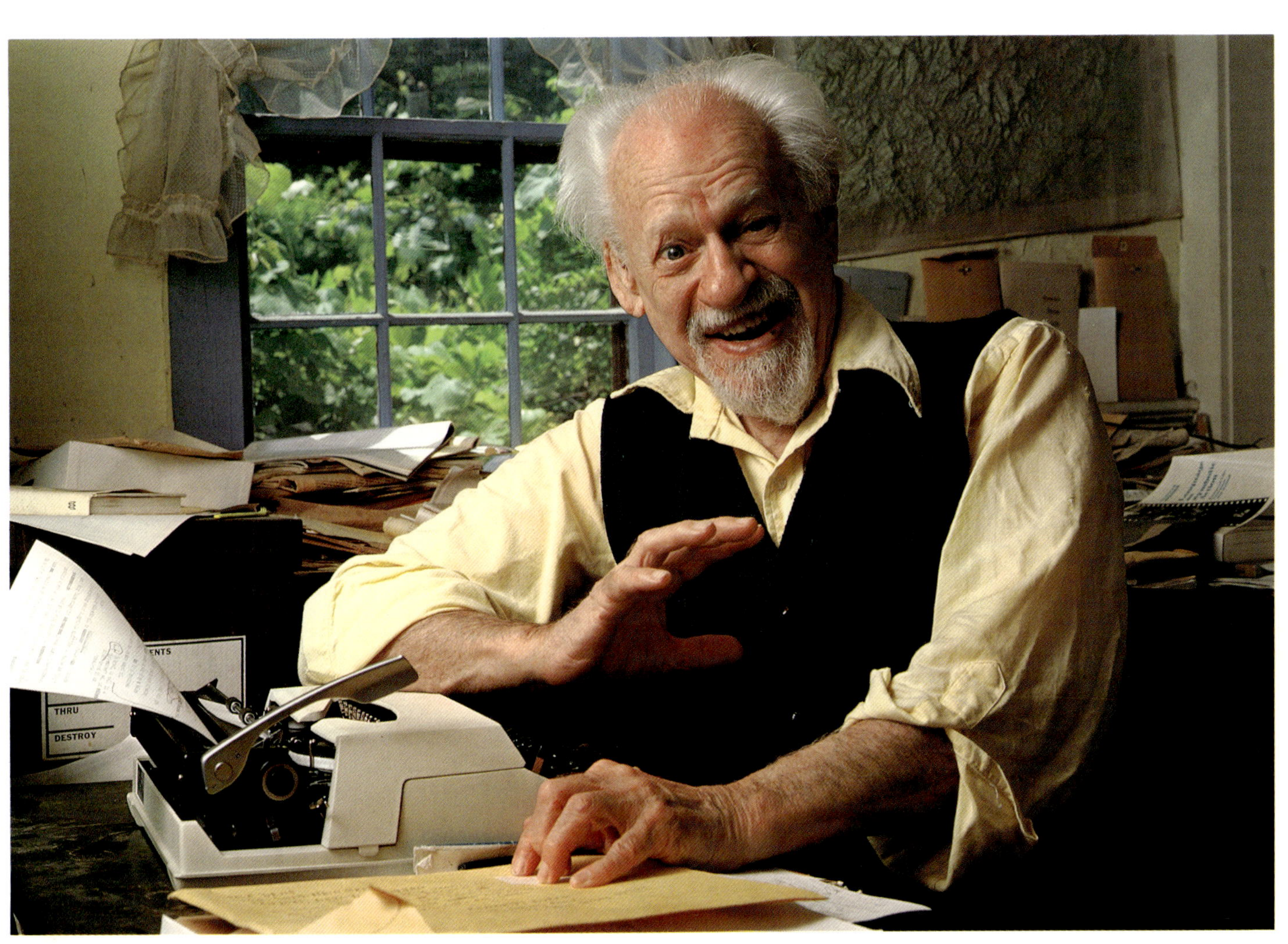
THRU
DESTROY

Acknowledgments

I have had the unique and special privilege of meeting a group of people united by age who have been an inspiration to me, and I want to thank them—beautiful octogenarians all—for their time, energy, and interest.

Thank-yous must also go to the people who have helped me in a variety of important ways: To Barbara Lyons, for getting the ball rolling; to Heidi Steffens, for the words that fill these pages; and to Phyllis Freeman, for adding the finishing touches. And thank you, Raphael.

To Ellen Buchalter, Carol Weber, Michael Lasky, Susan Gold, Eddie Mandelbaum, Gerry Speno, Judy Licht, and Kay Berkson, thank you for your generosity. Special thanks to my sister, Judy, and to Howard Wechsler of the Orchid Restaurant.

For assorted favors and assistance, thank you, Vic Mazurkiewicz, Avis Berman, Irwin Buchalter, Claude Levy, Harold Silverman, Bill Price, Denise Collier, and Aunt Gloria.

And finally I want to thank my friend and fellow photographer Marty Umans, for planting the idea for this book in my head.

N. R. S.